TRAINING FOR EQUALITY
A Study of Race Relations and Equal Opportunities Training

Colin Brown
Jean Lawton

POLICY STUDIES INSTITUTE
100 PARK VILLAGE EAST, LONDON NW1 3SR

The publishing imprint of the independent
POLICY STUDIES INSTITUTE
100 Park Village East, London NW1 3SR
Telephone: 071-387 2171; Fax: 071-388 0914

© Crown copyright 1991.

ISBN 0 85374 526 9 (Discussion Paper 33)
A CIP catalogue record of this book is available from the British Library.
1 2 3 4 5 6 7 8 9

How to obtain PSI publications
All book shop and individual orders should be sent to PSI's distributors:
BEBC Ltd, 9 Albion Close, Parkstone, Poole, Dorset, BH12 3LL

Books will normally be despatched in 24 hours. Cheques should be made payable
to BEBC Ltd.

Credit card and telephone/fax orders may be placed on the following freephone
numbers:

FREEPHONE: 0800 262260 FREEFAX: 0800 262266

Booktrade Representation (UK & Eire)
Book Representation Ltd
P O Box 17, Canvey Island, Essex SS8 8HZ

PSI Subscriptions
PSI Publications are available on subscription.
Further information from PSI's subscription agent:
Carfax Publishing Company Ltd
Abingdon Science Park, P O Box 25, Abingdon OX10 3UE

Laserset by Policy Studies Institute
Printed in Great Britain by Billing & Sons Ltd, Worcester

Contents

Preface

This report is based on a research project funded by the Employment Department. All views expressed are those of the authors and may not necessarily reflect those of the Employment Department.

We are grateful to Dennis Brooks of the Employment Department for his help and advice throughout the project. At PSI Jim Knox and Rex Baron gave us considerable practical assistance.

Our sincere thanks go to the many trainers and other people working in the field of race equality who gave us their time and shared their experiences and ideas with us.

Summary

1 Introduction

This research project aimed to take stock of the provision of race relations training and to establish the extent to which it meets current needs. The research comprised four elements: a review of the literature on race relations training and closely related subjects; interviews with providers of race relations training and with representatives of prominent organisations interested in race equality; interviews with representatives of organisations where there had been race relations training; and a telephone survey of a general sample of large firms, to discover whether they were engaged in any race relations or equal opportunities training and to gather other information about their staff training needs. There were 197 informants in the interview surveys and 125 informants in the telephone survey. The research included all types of employer in the public and private sectors, and concentrated on London (and its surrounding counties), the East and West Midlands, and West Yorkshire.

2 Review of the literature

The literature review is concerned with employee training relating to race relations in Britain over the last 20 years. The first section summarises the six best overviews of the subject (Peppard 1980, McIlroy 1981, Shaw 1982, Peppard 1983, Lee 1987 and Commission for Racial Equality 1987) and the second section discusses some of the more important themes and issues of the literature.

Themes and issues

Aims: It is useful to make a distinction between long-term and short-term aims; between training to reduce discrimination and positive action training; and between training for service delivery and for employment. There seems to be no disagreement about the overall aim of reducing discrimination and disadvantage suffered by minority ethnic groups, but the shorter-term objectives have varied a great deal.

The various short-term aims can be listed as: imparting cultural information to prevent misunderstandings at work; imparting cultural information to enable service delivery staff to take account of different ethnic groups needs; making people aware of the history and mechanisms of racism and discrimination, and helping them to develop strategies to oppose racial injustice; making people aware of racism underlying their own attitudes and behaviour, and helping them to develop strategies to deal with it; uncovering racist attitudes and trying to change them; developing skills and work practices designed to stop discrimination in personnel management; developing skills and practices designed to stop discrimination in service delivery; explaining the meaning of an organisation's equal opportunities programme and the duties that it puts on individuals; explaining the race relations legislation and its implications for the organisation and for the individual.

The literature reveals a trend in the race training field, beginning with an emphasis on cultural and legal information, moving through a period of interest in changing employees' attitudes, and then to a period of emphasis on procedures and duties. Throughout there is an argument about whether it is best to attempt changes in attitudes or changes in behaviour.

Needs and Evaluation: Authors stress the importance of tailoring training to the needs of organisations, and of examining the results of training. Evaluation is acknowledged to be difficult, because it is hard to separate the effects of training from those of other equal opportunities measures. Typically, post-course questionnaires have been used to judge the impact of training.

Racism Awareness Training: This subject has generated a great deal of discussion. Our account takes as its starting point the 'White Awareness' programme designed in the USA by Judy Katz. Emphasising individual change, the programme of exercises tackles the contradiction between people's words and actions, and the gap between constitutional ideals and the reality of racism. Katz's programme influenced developments in Britain in the early 1980s but soon attracted criticism from the political left, from the media, and from others working in race relations using different methods. From trainers, most of the criticism related to the unproven link between the 'conversion' of individual attitudes and changes in organisational practice. Despite the apparent retreat of RAT after these debates, it appears that its more useful elements have been incorporated into the eclectic body of methods and ideas used by trainers.

Practical issues

Levels of staff: training has embraced a growing spectrum of staff as the cultural awareness perspective has given way to an emphasis on discrimination, and as the focus has widened to cover employment as well as service delivery. *Relationship with other training*: the impression is that race relations training owes little to other types of training for its theory and methods, but it may simply be an unacknowledged debt. As regards integration with organisations' other training programmes, the balance seems to favour stand-alone courses. *Techniques*: exercises, discussions and workshops now form the backbone of training methods, although there is more substantive learning content than might be expected from this description. *Organisational context*: training approaches are more successful when the are rooted in the professional and social worlds of the trainees. Race relations training also needs to be part of a larger process of change in an organisation. The importance of individual follow-up after the courses is also emphasised.

3 Equal opportunities, business efficiency and training
Different organisations, different approaches

During the interviews we found a considerable variety of approaches to race relations and equal opportunities training. In most organisations the training has emerged from a general management effort against discrimination, beginning with an equal opportunities policy of some sort. It is helpful to recognise a dichotomy between justice-oriented approaches and efficiency-oriented approaches: it is clear that some organisations have started from a formal political commitment while others have been strongly influenced by fears of recruitment shortages and doubts about ethnic minority markets.

Demand in different sectors

It is clear from our interviews with trainers that up to now the majority of paying customers have been in the public sector and the voluntary sector.

Most of the private-sector firms with a strong equality effort are well known and our research has not extended the list a great deal. A number of large employers with a history of equal opportunities considerations in their employment practices have been joined by others, principally in the financial sector and the media. The telephone survey was carried out in order to give some indications of the mood among a more general sample of larger private sector employers. It revealed very little specific training on race relations, although there is a fairly widespread recognition that good personnel practices require a training input with equal opportunities as part of it.

In the private sector the existence of equal opportunities policies and equal opportunities training seems to be strongly related to the size of firms. Both the interviews and the telephone survey showed that they were found more often in larger firms.

Why do organisations seek equal opportunities training?

In very simple terms, organisations are seeking one or more of the following results from race relations training: to get equal opportunities change moving; to give a signal that things are moving; to develop a strategy; to win over key staff; or to deliver technical advice, information and skills.

Who takes the decisions?

Usually the overall equal opportunities policy is established at a high level within an organisation but the real choices about training are taken at lower levels, by personnel managers, departmental managment, special working parties or outside consultants. In the private sector, the equal opportunities training is usually organised by a manager in the training or personnel department. Some firms have appointed an equal opportunities manager with responsibility for training in this area. In local authorities the situation is similar to that in the private sector, although managers and units with special responsibility for equal opportunities are more common. High-level decisions about equal opportunities tend to have a more detailed content in local authorities.

In the charitable and voluntary sector the decisions over equal opportunities matters, including training, tend to be taken at directorial or managing council level, but also involve consultation with staff.

The importance of general training arrangements
Nearly all of the organisations with equal opportunities training already had substantial general training programmes for their staff.

Organisational change and individual duties
Some organisations use training to facilitate the development of policy for equality, while others use it to equip individual staff to do their jobs better. Voluntary and charitable bodies tend to start with training aimed at substantial organisational overhaul.

Initial training efforts tend to concern awareness or general concepts of equal opportunity, and concentrate on senior staff or middle-grade staff, while training later turns to more practical issues such as recruitment and selection, and for staff at lower levels. In all sectors the training for staff comprises a mixture of duty-oriented and discretion-oriented content, the balance between the two often depending on the nature of the organisation and the job in question.

4 Provision of race related training
Race relations training has been provided through a number of different channels. They can be grouped as follows:
   (i) Publicly-funded services: Race Relations Employment Advisory Service; Industrial Language Training Units; Commission for Racial Equality; Race Equality Councils; other publicly funded training services.
   (ii) Independents: independent training consultancies; independent freelance trainers.
   (iii) Associations: public employers' organisations; professional associations.
   (iv) Labour movement: TUC; individual trade unions.
   (v) In-house: organisations' own internal training sections.

Training courses on the market
Some courses are arranged for staff of a single organisation and others are open to people from more than one. The diversity of 'courses' should not be underestimated. Within this diversity it is hard to judge in what form the largest volume of race relations training has taken place – but our work suggests that courses in fair recruitment and selection take precedence, followed by those on equality of service delivery.

The most common length of the discrete courses on recruitment and selection, or on awareness, is two to three days, although one-day courses are not uncommon. Courses extending beyond a week are rare, although some are broken up into sections over several months adding to more than a week in total.

Training and equal opportunities consultancy
Most of the providers feel that it is important to combine their equal opportunities training with other organisational development work and other staff development work.

Course design and assessing training needs
Most trainers like to spend some time studying an organisation before recommending a training course and other measures. In some cases this assessment is possible, where an employer accepts the value of the exercise and resources are available. Trainers said that most organisations do not have the level of commitment required for this. Typically, trainers instead have an initial meeting with a manager or personnel officer, then another after a more detailed training plan has been developed, and perhaps one or two other meetings with key staff.

Costs
RREAS make no charges for their services. The CRE and the RECs do a small amount of training work within single organisations, and have no fixed charging policy. Most of the independents explained that they charge a daily rate per trainer; often the actual rate is negotiable. For the majority of trainers, daily rates per trainer in the public sector were between £200 and £300; a small number, however, started at £500 or more per trainer (these are all 1988 prices). The top end of the scale was, for the majority of trainers, less than £600 per day. For open courses there was a charge per trainee, and again we found a wide range, from under £40 per day to over £150 per day.

The implications of different funding arrangements
The fact that organisations are comparatively reluctant to pay for extensive consultancy in the run-up to training means that publicly funded and grant funded trainers have had greater flexibility than independent trainers; background funding permits a greater input of non-training hours.

Networks and individuals
It would be wrong to visualise the independent sector of training provision as being neatly made up of consultancies with permanent full-time staff, operating independently of and in competition with individual freelance trainers. The consultancies tend to employ people who themselves do freelance work or who have permanent part-time jobs elsewhere.

Marketing
The consensus among the independent trainers is that standard advertising methods have little effect. Most business comes by recommendation or by repeat orders.

Selecting trainers
Organisations seeking training have to rely on a variety of formal and informal sources of information. The most common starting point is enquiry among professional contacts. Over half the consumers considered more than one provider before taking them on. In the private sector, our informants suggested that the financial arguments about equal opportunities training centred on its contribution to saving money, rather than worries about its cost. Some, however, commented that one factor that made RREAS attractive was the fact that their services are free.

The training effort
The main areas covered by the courses have been: general equal opportunities concepts and strategies of change; awareness of racism and discrimination; fair recruitment and selection; personnel policy and practice; ethnic monitoring principles and procedures; and equality in public service delivery. Common to most courses is an attempt to give a conceptual framework and language to deal with the ideas of racism, discrimination and equality of opportunity. Most of the race relations employment training has been among managers, supervisors and personnel staff. Training with a service delivery emphasis has more often taken in staff from lower levels.

What is available?
The array of available courses for race relations training does not represent a plethora of different approaches to the same objective;

rather, it reflects the variety of aims which training is employed to pursue. Trainers tend to offer a range of services but also have their own specialisms.

Content of typical courses

Despite the variety of training available, there is a surprising degree of convergence of course content for each training objective. To illustrate this, the report lists a typical programme for each of three types of training: recruitment and selection, company equal opportunities policy, and general anti-discrimination and equal opportunity practices for service providers.

Training methods

Most equal opportunities training is now based on a mixture of methods, with an emphasis on the value of group work and self-discovery. Courses tend to be based on groups of eight to fifteen trainees, most commonly with two trainers. Different courses are run for different levels of staff.

Many of the trainers use video films to trigger some of the discussions, but they play down the importance of the content of particular videos. Consumers of equal opportunities training seem to give a higher value to video content. Collections of written training materials are built up by individual trainers and agencies. Trainers again play down the importance of the content, saying that they are just props to facilitate interpersonal processes.

Most of the trainers we spoke to felt that courses are more effective if an ethnic minority trainer is involved, although many spoke of the pitfall of setting minority trainers the impossible task of representing black people to the course.

All the trainers said they sometimes encounter difficulties with course participants. The sensitivity of the subject matter means that individuals and groups can feel threatened and respond disruptively. In general, however, trainers say these problems are not serious obstacles to achieving training objectives.

5 Measuring outcomes

Many trainers and clients suggested that the training in which they were involved had not been 'properly' evaluated. Their view was that direct evaluation is feasible but they have been unable to do it; we argue in this chapter that, on the contrary, direct evaluation is not feasible, but the evaluation tools already in use are of value. It is practicable to evaluate the extent to which particular training courses achieve some of their short-term aims, but not their long-term equality outcomes; and it is practicable to evaluate outcomes of overall equal opportunity programmes, but not the special contribution that the training makes to these.

The contribution of individual trainers
As with any course that relies on people to engage with participants on difficult issues, success is dependent on the skills, experience and abilities of the trainers.

External and internal trainers
The jolt that training can give to an organisation is more effective, according to some informants, if the trainers are from outside. However, outside trainers do sometimes have problems of unfamiliarity with the organisation.

Clients' appraisal of the training
The difficulties of direct evaluation mean that it is hard to give exact answers about the contribution of training to the equality efforts of the organisations we visited, but it is our strong impression that the training has, in the majority of cases, had a beneficial outcome in terms of the development and implementation of equal opportunity programmes. There were few examples of training going badly wrong, and in those cases other training measures were taken to put matters right.

Indicators of overall equality performance of organisations were mentioned by informants as showing, at least in part, the effect of training. Some informants made less specific comments about the improvements that race relations training have led to. For voluntary and community organisations, and to some extent in local authority departments, one result of race-related training seems to be a change in their dealings with white clients: staff are more likely to make a stand against racial abuse, harassment and exclusion. Sometimes another result of race related training and associated programmes is a heightened sense of identity among ethnic minority employees.

6 Aiming for equality
Training and organisational change
'Race relations and equal opportunities training' refers not to a single type of employee training but embraces a wide range of activities. The diversity of training packages reflects a real diversity of needs and training aims; this analysis stands in contrast to the view that the diversity of training results from a confused set of approaches to a single training aim.

Establishing training aims
In practice, the process by which organisations choose from the options has not been uniform, but we can see regularities within different categories of organisation, sometimes resulting from the direction of pressure for change, and sometimes in line with the nature of the client organisation or department.

The training aims must rest on an assessment of two things: first, the present shortcomings of equality performance, and second, the changes necessary to improve that performance. Depending on these assessments, a 'training' programme can be established with the right balance of organisational development, consultancy, high-level workshops, and staff training of different types.

In the main, organisations are satisfied with the quality of training, but there have been problems when the training objectives have been unclear or simply wrong for the organisation, and when training is expected to carry the entire burden of change. The important question is not whether equal opportunities training as such is any good, but this: what types of training are necessary and appropriate?

Promoting investment in equal opportunities
Another practical issue is the relationship between what an organisation needs and what it is prepared to do. In the private sector we were told repeatedly that a business reason is required, and that a simple argument about justice has little effect. Many said that they were prompted to think about their recruitment procedures by a shortage or by the fear of shortages to come. Another business-oriented motivation for equality measures is the realisation of ethnic minority markets. Some employers are also concerned to avoid trouble with the Race Relations Act.

   The larger companies that have set out to improve their equality performance do say that 'public image' is one of the factors that prompted them, and that a momentum develops in a particular industry. Responsibility for the growth of that momentum rests both in the organisations that have made some progress already, and among those who can convince employers of the business advantages of equal opportunities change and of the need for fairness and justice.

1 Introduction

Race relations training

This is the report of a research project set up to take stock of the provision of employee race relations training and to establish the extent to which it meets current needs. The study included all types of employer in both public and private sectors. Our research work therefore took us to manufacturing firms, local authorities, banks and building societies, government departments, charities, voluntary organisations and a variety of other organisations, all of whom have been involved in some way with employee training in the area of race relations. As the report makes clear, the term race relations training is an umbrella term for a large variety of activities. Often it is provided as part of a wider programme on equal opportunities and is termed equal opportunities training. In practice there is no consensus on what should be called race relations training and what should be called equal opportunities training, and we have therefore not attempted to impose strict definitions of our own. The scope of this report includes training that goes beyond issues of race equality, but race equality issues are its starting point and we do not cover training that is exclusively concerned with other equality issues.

The PSI study

The research work for the PSI study comprised four elements:

(1) A review of the literature on race relations training and closely related subjects. This forms the next chapter of the report, and a bibliography is appended.
(2) A round of 95 interviews with providers of race relations training and with 15 interviews with representatives of prominent organisations interested in race equality.
(3) A round of 87 interviews with representatives of organisations where race relations training had been organised for employees.
(4) A telephone survey of a general sample of 125 large firms.
   All of the interviews were carried out in 1988 and 1989.

The interviews for parts (2) and (3) were intended to obtain the views of providers on the one hand and of consumers on the other. In practice, the training world does not divide so easily in this way. A number of large organisations arrange their own equal opportunities training in-house, and therefore cannot be simply classified as one or the other. Even where independent trainers come into an organisation, the in-house trainers sometimes assist with the course. In some cases organisations are providers of training to others, but have themselves had training from outsiders. In the end the classification we use is not as important as the substance of what people had to say, and there is some value in the fact that a number of informants had a perspective from both sides of the fence.

Interviews with providers

In this phase of the project we carried out interviews with two main groups of people. The first group comprised providers of training, many of whom were freelance trainers or groups of trainers operating as independent companies, although some others (such as the Department of Employment Race Relations Employment Advisory Service (RREAS), the Industrial Language Training (ILT) units and trainers in the trade union movement) were wholly or partly funded by public bodies or by parent bodies. The second group was a mixture of people from organisations that were involved with race training mainly at arm's length, or were generally important in the area of race relations and equal opportunities. As with the distinction between providers and consumers, there are some problems of definition: some of the organisations we approached for a general view turned out to be providing some actual training.

We built up a list of providers of training from a number of sources: some people and organisations were already known to us professionally; the Local Government Training Board (LGTB) published a directory of individuals and organisations offering training, and from this we extracted the names of those working in the field of race and equal opportunities; discussions with contacts at the Commission for Racial Equality (CRE) and the Local Authorities Race Relations Information Exchange (LARRIE) added more names, as did our monitoring of course advertisements; and during all our interviews in this phase of the project we sought information on trainers that we might otherwise have missed. We are confident that few organisations offering training specifically in this field escaped our notice.

Most of the names of the list were to be found in or around the geographical areas chosen for emphasis in the third phase of the project, and we therefore decided to concentrate on those areas: London (and its surrounding counties), the East and West Midlands, and West Yorkshire. This emphasis was not applied rigidly, however, and we went elsewhere to see trainers whom we considered to be particularly interesting. We approached all the organisations on our list in the appropriate areas; there were few refusals, although some interviews were difficult to achieve because of trainers' very full diaries.

In most cases the interviews with trainers were with individuals, (individual freelance trainers or representatives of organisations) but in some cases we had discussions with groups of people from organisations; occasionally these were convened as ad-hoc seminars. Generally the response from the trainers was good, and some helped us a great deal. The initial reactions were sometimes cautious, but careful explanation of the purpose of the project and assurances of confidentiality usually secured co-operation. Often the main concern of trainers was to know whether we understood the background issues of racism and discrimination. The interviews mostly lasted between one and two-and-a-half hours; a few were shorter and a few were much longer. Some trainers were keen to talk for a long time, occasionally over more than one meeting.

In all the total number of people whom we interviewed on the provision side was 95, and the total number of people 'at arm's length', who provided no training, was 15. These figures exclude the people we spoke to in local authorities, whom we included in part (3) of the study, described below.

Interviews with consumers

Using several methods we built up a list of organisations in the study areas (London, the East and West Midlands, and West Yorkshire) that had arranged race relations training for their staff. First we approached a number of local authorities that we knew, from previous contacts and publicly available information, to have mounted training in equal opportunities. Then we asked the appropriate informants from the providers survey for lists of past clients; few refused on principle, and although obtaining the actual lists was difficult in practice, we did eventually receive a substantial number of names of organisations in this way. Then we approached a further group of organisations we knew to have made some effort on equal opportunities training, using information from our own professional contacts and attendance at various meetings and seminars. Our main objective in putting together the sample of organisations for this part of the study was breadth of experience and sector. It was easy to find public sector organisations where there had been training, but much harder in the private sector. The final sample contained a good variety of organisations from all sectors.

In this part of the study we interviewed 87 people from about 70 organisations; we say 'about 70' because a small number of the organisations were related to each other (as subsidiaries, for instance) and cannot strictly be said to be separate organisations, even though they do have rather different experiences of equal opportunities training.

The telephone survey of large firms

The purpose of the telephone survey was to contact a random sample of large private sector employers to discover whether they were engaged in any training in race relations or equal opportunities, and to gather other information about their staff training needs. We used a sample generated from a commercial database of business records collected direct from companies and from information kept at Companies House. We selected organisations that employed at least 100 people and were in the same geographical areas as our interviews with trainers and consumers.

We restricted the sample to large companies because we did not expect many small companies to be actively pursuing equal opportunities strategies, and thought they would be very unlikely to have any related training. As small firms make up the vast majority of companies, the survey would have shown very little indeed had we not imposed this lower size limit.

We completed 125 telephone interviews (a response rate of 66 per cent). The interviews lasted between five minutes and twenty minutes. The interview schedule is shown at the end of the report.

2   Review of the Literature

This review and the appended bibliography are primarily concerned with employee training in matters relating to race relations in Britain over the last 20 years. The use of the term 'employee' here includes people working at all levels: as we shall see, in many cases employees in management grades have been the recipients of training as well as shop-floor workers and office staff. The aim of this review is to provide a short guide to the development of race relations training in Britain and to the debates over principles and practice. The first section summarises the six best overviews of the subject and the second section discusses some of the more important themes and issues of the literature.

Overviews
The bibliography lists many articles, reports and books dealing with race relations training, but a few of them are particularly useful for an overview of developments in Britain over the last 20 years. They are:
   Peppard 1980
   McIlroy 1981
   Shaw 1982
   Peppard 1983
   Lee 1987
   Commission for Racial Equality 1987

Peppard 1980. This article was the first general look at the British race relations training scene. It argued that the provision was fragmented and that the whole subject received insufficient research and analysis. It called for an attempt to be made 'to formulate a rationale and some training models appropriate to this country', and ended with the warning that 'this is an area in which we can no longer afford to be amateurs.'

Peppard observed that so far training had been based on two premises: (i) that training was needed only for 'practitioner services' (that is, only in relation to service delivery) and (ii) that its aim was to improve the practitioners' understanding of minority communities. The narrowness of this perspective of 'multicultural awareness' was, however, beginning to be recognised, with teacher training moving away from education for immigrant children and towards education for a multiracial society, and with the police and other agencies turning to consider issues of racial prejudice.

Peppard suggested that the practical objective of race relations training for employees should be 'to enable staff to carry out their particular duties with equity and maximum efficiency.' She suggested the necessary elements as (a) a common core of historical, psychological, legal and cultural background information, combined with (b) other subjects tailored to the particular occupational group. The second element should take on the issues of institutional racism and challenge attitudes and belief within the context of professional conduct:

> A practical analysis of what is required clearly shows that those attitudes or beliefs which underlie actual behaviour must be seen as the heart of the matter and that to construct a training scheme which tries to ignore them is to beg the question.

Peppard classed training methods under three headings: didactic methods, groupwork methods and experiential methods. Didactic methods are those involving traditional teaching by a lecturer, and there have been mixed reports of their efficacy in reducing prejudice: Peppard cited research by Miller (1969) which suggested that lectures and discussions can reinforce racialist attitudes rather than erode them, but she also cited later work by Bagley and Verma (1978) which suggested that teaching 'may well be beneficial in reducing prejudice' and at least does no harm. Peppard noted that much depends on the qualities of the lecturer, and on the extent to which the teaching can be rooted in the social world of the trainees. Groupwork techniques (such as those involving small group discussions, role playing and training games) have their origins in mainstream management training. In 1980 these techniques were not widely used for race relations training in Britain, except in the early developments around the idea of racism awareness training. Training that aimed to tackle attitudes about race had been gathering pace in the USA, in several federal organisations and in the armed forces; in particular, Judy Katz had developed her 'White Awareness' programme at the University of Oklahoma. Experiential techniques are those which aim to modify prejudiced attitudes by inter-ethnic personal contact: by 'meeting, mixing, living and working with members of other ethnic groups.' Peppard noted that American research had, for example, shown a decline in prejudice after desegregation in housing, and that informal evidence suggested some success of the training technique in Britain. American trainers, however, had pointed to a problem (one that recurs in the literature) concerning the difficult position of the black people in such encounters: experiential training puts the responsibility for creating change on their shoulders.

Looking to the future, she pointed to some problems that would stand in the way of a simple application of American methods in this country, problems rooted in the different histories of race relations and different use of language. She also drew attention to the uncertain nature of the connection between individual prejudice and discrimination by organisations, suggesting that the issue was important to a clarification of the aims of race relations training. Calling for an assessment of what behaviour is meant to be influenced by training, the article asked:

> Is it face-to-face dealings with ethnic minorities (e.g. by police officers, teachers, social workers), is it administrative procedures which will affect minorities, is it decision-making by high level policy-makers? If we can identify the areas where we think there is a danger of non-equitable or unjust behaviour by holders of key roles, we could move forward from that knowledge to discovering the perceptions, the information and the attitudes which underlie the specific behaviour.

McIlroy 1981. This article looked specifically at industry, welcoming the growth since the mid-1970s in the provision of race relations training and education for management and trade unions. Courses (or special components of more general courses) were run by employers, individual unions, the Trades Union Congress (TUC), the Industrial Training Boards (ITBs), the Industrial Language Training Units (ILTUs) and the Commission for Racial Equality (CRE), falling into three categories: those for immigrants, dealing with communication and technical matters; those for black and white workers together, to ease integration, and largely dealing with communication; and those for managers and union officials, largely about race relations in a broader sense, ranging from patterns of immigration to action on equal opportunities. The article focused on the third type of training – courses involving white decision-makers, which provide an opportunity for dealing with white racialism.

McIlroy noted that an influential approach to such courses at the time was to stick to the provision of technical information regarding race relations and the relevant legislation, and he argued that the approach leaves the prejudices of trainees untouched, or makes an unwarranted assumption that there are no such problems. Furthermore, there is a danger that the isolated provision of detailed information about the law may enable people to continue discriminating with less chance of being caught. McIlroy also warned that concentrating on the suggested solutions to the problem without an analysis of the problem itself could lead to a superficial compliance with the principles of equal opportunities without real commitment. As an example of the general approach, he cited the Rubber and Plastics ITB publication *Managing in the Multi-Racial Company* (RPITB, 1979), which dealt with many aspects of the legislation and equal opportunities but referred only once to prejudice and discrimination: that reference was to the problem of 'British workers no longer applying for jobs when workers of ethnic minorities are employed' – in other words, discrimination by job applicants, not by anyone in a position of power.

McIlroy questioned whether the accumulated experience of mainstream management training was a real resource for the development of race relations training in Britain, as Peppard had suggested. His view was that management training was too concerned with 'maximising the existing organisational position within an economic and social status quo', and that effective race relations training might require an approach that was too challenging to this managerial paradigm.

The article went on to consider the more sophisticated and increasingly common courses that anticipated the racialist ideas of trainees and sought to change them. McIlroy pointed out that a problem often existed with this approach:

> ...many industrial tutors who accept this conception seem to operate on a rather simplistic conversion-process model in which the attitudes of students are transformed by a mix of 'the facts', patient rational

argument and the practical problems that they encounter in role play or case studies.

Racially prejudiced attitudes and behaviour are rather more complex than is suggested by this approach, and they usually exist within a framework of powerful influences in the workplace – influences much stronger than the effect of the 'cleansing' race relations course. The correct approach, McIlroy argued, should be more comprehensive than any to date, and the term 'education and training' would be an improvement: courses should incorporate more difficult subject matter with the straightforward information. He also argued that we should not expect to be able to eliminate racialist ideas held by trainees, but merely to open their eyes and start the process of questioning. Finally he called for more resources for race relations training and education, and for it to be seen as only part of 'an overall strategy of social change aimed at eradicating the roots of racialism'.

Shaw 1982. This article lamented the lack of unified philosophy and methodology behind race relations training, and behind its predecessor human relations training. It reviewed the techniques used in race relations training, drawing mainly (but not wholly) on US experience, and employing a distinction between 'content techniques', which aimed to impart information, and 'process techniques', which aimed to improve attitudes and skills. The distinction came from human relations training; in an earlier article he had noted that Peppard's use of the term 'didactic methods' corresponded to the content techniques of human relations training, and her 'groupwork' and 'experiential' methods corresponded to process techniques (Shaw, 1980).

Looking first at attempts at total organisational change, Shaw discussed the examples of the US Army and the US Health Services and Mental Health Association (HSMHA). He pointed out that there were no UK examples to date. In 1972 the US Army began a programme which included compulsory 'in-house' awareness training at all levels, as well as policy changes. A built-in evaluation programme revealed that during the first two years of the programme there were improvements in the career advancement of black soldiers and in racial harmony, partly as a result of the measures taken. But subsequently those improvements tailed off, leaving blacks still in a substantially disadvantaged position, and the evaluation research showed that at army unit level the training was often poor and commitment to it was weak: 'This case study shows that positive trends stabilised and improvement was halted as organisational commitment to the change programme declined.' Shaw cited the HSMHA as an example of successful change. Top management initiated a programme which began with the circulation of the equal opportunity objectives to all staff; the number of equal opportunities officers was increased, and they were involved in all appointments and promotions; equal opportunities councils were established; and all management staff were given three-day residential training courses on equal opportunities, based mainly on multi-ethnic groupwork, with a small amount of conventional teaching. An evaluation was carried out which showed that the programme led to 'marked improvements in equal opportunity.'

Shaw noted that most training schemes related to race have been pitched at a level less than a whole organisation – usually a small group or individual level. He stressed the value of conventional, substantive teaching on race and equal opportunities issues (content techniques), but argued that the motivation of trainees was of great importance, and that variations in this factor explained the contradictions among the earlier research findings (e.g. Miller vs Bagley and Verma). The adverse reaction by trainees who did not perceive a need for the training had been observed with a range of different methods, and not just with the content techniques. Shaw also stressed the importance of the trainer's credibility – trainers are most successful when they have understanding of and experience in the professional world of the trainee group. Process techniques were also reviewed in the article, but with less firm conclusions. Shaw considered evidence about the value of multi-ethnic discussion groups and role-playing, and although some successes were reported, other studies were less encouraging, and the results of nearly all were ambiguous.

He pointed to the combination of content and process techniques as the best way forward, and gave Katz's white awareness programme as a fruitful example of such a synthesis. He suggested that content and process should be balanced to reflect the needs of the particular organisation and trainees.

Shaw said that three fundamental questions arose from his review. First, whether there was any future in training programmes that were not tied to schemes for organisational change: he felt that there was not. The second question was whether training could be designed to minimise an adverse reaction from white people: whilst unable to answer to this, Shaw pointed out that work on the US Army indicated that the damaging effects of any adverse reaction were balanced by the greater commitment shown by other trainees to equality and equal opportunity measures. The third question was whether the methods developed so far amounted to 'a sound basis on which to proceed.' He concluded that they did, but that the planning of training needed to become much more specific to the trainees' jobs.

Peppard 1983. In this article the considerable progress in the early 1980s was documented, and the contributions of many organisations and individuals were recorded. Peppard noted that in the absence of any widely-available body of information on techniques and materials, much of the development had been from scratch and the only co-ordination of effort was on an informal basis. She argued that on balance this was a good thing at the time because it encouraged new ideas and led to imaginative experimentation.

After the Scarman Report on the trouble in Brixton in 1981, race training in the police force saw major developments (these proved to be very influential in the general evolution of training in Britain). A working party set up to look at community relations training reported in 1983, recommending a more comprehensive approach and more imaginative training, including groupwork. New courses for trainers and a pilot project on racism awareness training were set up. A major initiative was the establishment of a centre to advise on and assist with police training in community relations. Some forces had already begun to change their training methods. In particular, the Metropolitan Police had adopted elements of the Human Awareness Training programme developed at Patrick Air Force Base, Florida, covering interpersonal skills, community relations (including racism awareness) and self-awareness. Among the methods used were role-playing, games, exercises and the screening of videos. Meanwhile a series of annual seminars for senior officers of all forces had been running for several years at Holly Royde College of Manchester University.

Peppard listed a number of developments in other sectors, many of which reflected a diminishing emphasis on minority cultures and a growing interest in the ideas and methods of US-style racism awareness training. She pointed to training moves in the fields of education, social services, local authorities, the prison and probation services, industry and the civil service. Training was organised by a variety of bodies, some of them specialising in this field, such as the Racism Awareness Programme Unit and the Northern Race Training and Intervention Unit, while others offered race training as only part of their work.

The US military experience, as described by Shaw above, was considered in this article too. Peppard acknowledged that the different histories of race relations diminished the applicability of American lessons in the UK, but said that the US evaluation reports often gave British trainers 'a sense of deja vu.' She listed five points of concurrence of trainers' experience on both sides of the Atlantic: (1) a well-prepared training programme will produce some change for the better; (2) the training has to be geared to the occupational situation of the trainees; (3) training has to be built on, and backed up by the efforts of people in power in the organisation; (4) training is better if its focus is widened from issues of race alone to issues concerning other types of discrimination and disadvantage; (5) race relations training must be part of a wider programme promoting equal opportunities within the organisation.

Problems of a peculiarly British origin had emerged in relation to the involvement of black people in training and in relation to terminology. The inter-ethnic ('experiential') elements of courses were limited by the small number of black staff in most organisations, and many groups of trainees were all white, giving an 'us and them' flavour to course discussions. Terminology caused problems because of the changing fashions over words in the race relations field and the different meanings given by different social and political contexts. Commending Banton's discussion (1983) of this issue, Peppard stated:

> Trainers and other practitioners may well argue that they their control over the development of language is strictly limited and that they are constantly faced with fashionable usages and interpretations. Nevertheless, this kind of expert academic analysis is invaluable in reminding them of the importance of applying some rigour of thought to defining the premises on which they are constructing their training sessions.

The article also drew attention to three general questions: what is the primary aim of race relations training, what information should be got over to trainees, and how should training be evaluated? Should the primary aim be to change attitudes or to change behaviour?

Peppard's view was that the question itself is flawed: attitudes and behaviour are tied together in a way that makes their logical separation difficult to sustain. In practice, there are few jobs that really involve only 'playing it by the book', and most allow people a degree of discretion, and therefore even when people stick to the letter of their formal duties there is plenty of scope for prejudiced attitudes to find an outlet in discrimination. She also cites Southgate's research (1982) to argue that while it is very difficult to talk people out of their attitudes, training can make them sensitive to the impact of their language and non-verbal behaviour. The choice of what to include in the information element of courses is a more practical problem, because different occupations and different levels of seniority tend to demand different things: Peppard gave examples of social workers' need for cultural information and managers' need for information on the legislation and equal opportunities policy, and argued that the distinction between education and training is an important one in deciding what the balance should be between different types of information. Evaluation was the final issue considered in the article, but its importance was stressed:

> Uncomfortable as it may be for instructors and organisers, training will never achieve maximum effectiveness if a smooth routine, accompanied by the filling in by participants of what cynical trainers call 'happiness sheets' at the end of the course, is interpreted as success, and if methods and results are never questioned.

Lee 1987. This paper was a review of two categories of training aimed at promoting equality of opportunity: first, training for ethnic minority workers (such as English language training for Asian workers, access courses and other kinds of positive action training) and secondly, training for white workers aimed at reducing institutional racism and improving interpersonal relationships between blacks and whites. One of her main arguments was that the positive action variety of training had not received enough emphasis and that its development from 1981 onwards had been limited, fragmented and uneven, even when compared with race training for whites. She also pointed out that training provision had developed against a specific social and economic background: the pace of change had been affected by the recession (training budgets had been cut generally) and by the riots of the early 1980s (which gave a particular spur to race training for whites in public organisations).

As regards race training for white workers, Lee pointed out that employers took a variety of approaches, ranging from an emphasis on personnel management competence to attempts to change employees' attitudes towards ethnic minorities; trainers' approaches varied too, from the provision of cultural information through to the use of personal confrontation. For example, the Industrial Language Training Units stressed cultural information when first working with white workers but moved later towards awareness training. This move had not proved simple, meeting resistance from employers and trainees; it was acknowledged that attitudes could not be changed in a six-week course, but positive attitudes could be encouraged and negative ones could at the same time be disturbed. The ILTUs emphasised the importance of work with the trainees after the course.

The paper noted many of the developments in the field during the 1980s. Race relations training was being organised in a growing number of organisations: among teachers; in the health service; in the prison service; in the police; in the probation service; in local authorities; and elsewhere. Lee briefly described the work of the Racism Awareness Programme Unit, which provided training for a variety of bodies, mainly in the public and voluntary sectors. The ILTUs had by then broadened their work to cover race relations training in service delivery, and the Department of the Employment's Race Relations Employment Advisory Service had also expanded into training work. But Lee was critical of the absence of any co-ordinated national training policy, and of the fact that race training tended to happen only because of the interest and commitment of individual organisations. She also noted that innovation was easier for some organisations than for others: some, like trades unions, had to make courses attractive to their members to gain their interest, while 'a professional service or organisation where there is a lead from the top is in a stronger position to take a radical approach.' She also commented on the general under-representation of black trainers in the growth of training for whites.

While pointing out that training could contribute to the elimination of racism, Lee warned that there was a danger of it being seen as a panacea. She cautioned that it might be used as an easy option to allay fears about unrest and to placate consciences without challenging the status quo. She argued that race relations training could not in its own right achieve fundamental structural change in an organisation, and was only really effective as part of a general equal opportunity programme. This is a theme that emerges repeatedly in the literature. She was careful to point out what race relations training could do, however: it could hasten the implementation of changes, provide pressure to challenge the status quo, and attempt to shift attitudes. Training for ethnic minority workers – that is to say positive action training – could also enable them to operate more effectively, and to negotiate hurdles. A general equal opportunities effort within an organisation gave trainers greater authority and legitimacy in the eyes of trainees, while the training contributed to the general programme by providing a vehicle for heightening the awareness of managers and employees.

Commission for Racial Equality 1987. This publication is the CRE's current guide for employers seeking guidance about race-related training. It is in two volumes, the first dealing with issues of policy and planning and the second giving details of a number of cases studies, four from the UK and six from the USA and Canada. It is a practical guide rather than an academic review of developments, and it advises on good practice. It does, however, give brief and useful accounts of the various issues and arguments in the race training field. It concentrates on training for equal opportunities in the employment field and does not cover positive action training for ethnic minority employees or training for equality in service delivery.

The guide describes race-related training as covering four areas:

• providing information and advice on the implications of the relevant legislation and the Commission's Code of Practice;

• improving the ways in which both individuals and systems operate in a multi-racial society;

• increasing awareness of racism and prejudice, both at an individual and institutional level; and

• assisting staff to work in anti-racist ways.

It is stressed throughout that training should only be a part of a comprehensive equal opportunities strategy.

The guide lists the range of approaches that fall under the heading of race-related training: information sessions on the law and the Code of Practice; guidance on an organisation's equal opportunities policy and its practical application; guidance on discrimination and its elimination in practice; information on cultural differences and their implications; attitudinal training ('racism awareness'); and training for management and personnel skills for equal opportunities. There is also variety in length and intensity of training, which ranges from a single session to a course of several days. The CRE warns that actual training approaches are not always recognisable from course and programme titles:

> Phrases such as 'equal opportunity training,' 'race relations training,' 'racism awareness training,' 'multi-cultural awareness training' are used – often interchangeably – to cover a range of distinct activities...

Considering the debate over racism awareness training, the CRE gives a summary of the arguments put by proponents and opponents. It concludes with its own view that while the distinction between changing attitudes and changing behaviour is not as clear as it might appear at first, the fundamental aim of race-related training should be to 'contribute to the effective implementation of equal opportunity policies, ie the need to see a change in the behaviour of individuals and institutions,' and Katz-style racism awareness courses 'are thus not likely to play a major role in training programmes.' The guide states that training on 'cultural awareness' – on the background of the ethnic minority groups – can be helpful but care has to be taken that minority groups are not as a result portrayed as 'the problem.'

For organisations planning training, the CRE lists eight questions which it sees as key to an effective programme:
1. Why undertake training?
2. What needs analysis is required and what are the priority areas, by employee group?
3. What training and experience do the trainers require?
4. What are the objectives of each training session or programme?
5. What are the appropriate training methods and forms?
6. What is the relationship of race-related training to other training programmes?
7. How do training efforts interact with other steps the organisation should take to ensure effective implementation of its equal opportunity policy?
8. What evaluation needs to be undertaken?

The discussion of these questions in the CRE guide usefully draws together many of the problems mentioned by other authors and offers practical guidance on them. One point made clear is the need for preparation in advance of any race-related training: for an appropriate allocation of time and resources to gather information and analyse the needs of the organisation at different levels before launching into a programme of courses, and for preparation of the ground within the organisation – to ensure management support in particular. Part one of the guide concludes with a reminder that effective race-related training can only be of use within a context of a general equal opportunities programme.

The case studies give details of the training schemes adopted in a number of organisations and shows how those schemes have related to their general equality programmes. The British examples are Austin Rover, GEC, the London Borough of Hackney, and an un-named large utility company. The examples demonstrate the variety of training approaches in different organisations. In Austin Rover, the scheme comprised a short course (half a shift) for nearly 5,000 managers, staff and manual representatives. GEC in Leicester organised a comprehensive programme for many levels of staff, calling on the services of the Industrial Language Training Unit, the Engineering ITB and a management college. Hackney designed an in-house training scheme to cover all their staff. The utility company also arranged in-house training, but for personnel and management staff only.

Themes and issues

Several general points need to be made about the articles and books on training in the area of race. First, the arguments about training methods are sometimes carried out at a high level of abstraction when they would make more sense related to particular organisational settings. For example, the wisdom of training staff to understand ethnic minority cultures is a subject of some general debate, but the implications of such training differ between types of organisation: the advantages and disadvantages of multicultural awareness training for medical staff are not the same as for shop floor workers in industry, or for local authority personnel staff. Whilst practical and technical points should not become the arbiters of debates over aims and principles, those debates cannot fruitfully be carried on without proper regard for the practical repercussions in specific organisational settings.

The second general point is a caution against judging the early literature on the basis of the recent, more sophisticated arguments. The debates have developed at a rapid pace, and the use of some words and phrases has taken on an importance that did not exist before: to take an obvious example, the use of the term 'racism awareness' in Britain in the early 1980s would not necessarily have been intended to carry the same meaning as it would today. Some of the arguments about aims and strategies still spill over into arguments about terminology; this can obscure the real substance of the debate and the real character of the training methods involved.

The third general point is that some authors firmly locate the development of race training in the history of other race-related events and other general socio-economic developments, among them the recession, the urban riots and the political changes in local government. Others confine their analysis to the developments in the training field.

Fourth, it should be noted that the US experience has greatly influenced the literature on race training in this country; the impact on the development of training in practice has also been substantial. The area of biggest influence has been awareness training, but there have been others, and it is likely that the practical experience of American employers will continue to provide examples of programmes that are of interest here.

Aims
Some of the authors make explicit the aims of training as they see them, while others imply or assume aims. It is useful here to make a distinction between the overall aim towards which training is meant to make a contribution – that of reducing the discrimination and disadvantage suffered by minority ethnic groups – and the specific shorter-term objectives that might be achieved by training. There seems to be no real disagreement about the overall long-term aim, and there is therefore little to be gained from comparing its different formulations, but the shorter-term objectives have varied a great deal. This is clear from some of the titles: *Training to Integrate the Multiracial Workforce*; *The Effectiveness of Teaching Techniques for Reducing Colour Prejudice*; *The Employment of Black Social Workers – from 'ethnic sensitivity' to anti-racism*. We have already noted that Peppard (1980) saw the objective of training as enabling staff to do

their jobs with equity and efficiency, McIlroy (1981) saw it as dealing with white racism, and Lee (1987) saw it as reducing institutional racism and improving inter-ethnic relationships.

Many of the authors stress the importance of an overall organisational strategy to reduce the effects of racism and discrimination, within which training is only a part. This points to a distinction between race-related training and some other types of training: whether or not it involves increasing skills, it is unlike training for specific technical skills (such as for typing or for the use of machine tools) because it is directed at changing the functioning of the organisation, not merely at making the individual a more qualified employee. Many stress that training alone is unlikely to generate change, but different authors place different values on the importance of changes at the individual level and the organisational level.

Part of the general package of organisational change may be positive action training for ethnic minority employees or job applicants, and this is sometimes included in the definition of race relations training. Whether the label is appropriate or not does not really matter, but it is important to understand the distinction between the two types of training. Positive action training provides skills and knowledge to individuals to improve their own opportunities, while race relations training is aimed at people who can affect the opportunities of others, and seeks to reduce discrimination and other acts and mechanisms of racial bias by giving skills and knowledge or by changing attitudes.

Another important distinction is between training to improve equality performance in service delivery, such as in council housing provision and banking services, and training to improve an organisation's equality performance in employment and personnel matters. For example, race relations training in the US army has been personnel oriented, while training in British police forces has focused on dealing with the public; thus the main experiences of these two uniformed services are in two different types of training.

Returning to the analysis of the shorter-term objectives of race relations training, we can see that different authors identify a number of them:

• Imparting cultural information to prevent misunderstandings at work (O'Brien and Gubbay, 1979);

- Imparting cultural information to enable service delivery staff to take account of the different needs of different ethnic groups (HEC/NEC, 1984);

- Making people aware of the history and mechanisms of racism and discrimination, and helping them to develop strategies to oppose racial injustice (TUC, 1983);

- Making people aware of racism underlying their own attitudes and behaviour at work, and helping them to develop strategies to undermine that racism (Edmunds and Powell, 1985);

- Uncovering individual racist attitudes and trying to change them (Satow, 1982);

- Developing skills and encouraging work practices designed to stop discrimination against ethnic minorities in recruitment, promotion and other personnel practices (Carby and Thakur, 1977);

- Developing skills and encouraging work practices designed to stop discrimination against ethnic minorities in service delivery (Housing Training Project, 1980);

- Explaining the meaning of an organisation's equal opportunities programme and the duties that it puts on individuals in the organisation (Schneider, 1987);

- Explaining the race relations legislation and its implications both for the organisation and for the individual's own duties (CRE, 1987).

The literature reveals a general historical trend in the race training field which begins with an emphasis on cultural and legal information, moves through a period of interest in changing employees' attitudes, and then to a period where there is more emphasis on procedures and the duties of employees and managers. To some extent this trend has been the result of a gradual learning process among people working in the field, but it has also been accompanied by passionate debates over short-term aims and over methods. One of the central arguments has been about the relative importance of individuals' views and their actions at work. The debate over 'changing attitudes versus changing behaviour' revolves around a number of problems, including: the nature of racism; the mechanisms of discrimination; the strength and direction of the causal links between attitudes and behaviour; the malleability of personal attitudes; the extent of management control over the actions of individuals; the proper limits of an employer's concern with an employee's views and beliefs; and the connections between efficiency and equity of outcome. Many of these problems also emerge in the more specific argument over the training courses based on Judy Katz's white awareness programme, which we consider later.

Analysis of needs and evaluation of outcomes

Many of the sources point out that training has to be tailored to the needs of the organisation, and therefore an essential prerequisite for training is a 'needs analysis' to determine what its short-term aims should be. This is stressed by the writers who argue the importance of considering training as just one component of organisational change. Needs analysis is an area where an outside trainer's job spills over into general advice and help with equal opportunities.

Just as needs have to be examined, so do outcomes, but the evaluation of race relations training presents severe methodological problems. What measurable benefits are expected to emerge from the training? The answers depend partly on the long-term and short-term aims of the training, but they only lead us to further problems. If the long-term aim is (as we suggest is generally agreed) to reduce the discrimination and disadvantage suffered by people from ethnic minorities, then operational success should be gauged in terms of the achievement of targets and by other monitoring procedures. But that level of success will be the result of many things, and training is only one among them. Isolation of the precise contribution of training is not possible within a single organisation. If the short-term aims of training are concerned with individual change, then evaluating the real impact of the course is just as difficult: what constitutes an effective measure of change? 'Testing' people on the subject matter of the course is not the answer, because most people are capable of giving the 'correct answers' after a short course, irrespective of any lasting effect it may or may not have had. Evaluation has most commonly been considered in terms of changes in responses to batteries of attitude scales. This approach works on the assumption that the short-term aim of training is to produce a shift of attitudes, but even working with this assumption we can see there are difficulties in accepting an 'improvement' in scores as evidence of a real change in attitude, because once they have been on a course trainees may well give answers they know to be favoured. Another common approach is to ask trainees whether they think the training has been helpful and what they feel about different aspects of it. Whilst useful things can be learned from the comments of trainees, they cannot constitute an evaluation of whether the training has achieved its objectives.

An argument has been put forward that considerable attention is paid to the evaluation of race training while other sorts of training remain unassessed and unquestioned:

> ...realistically speaking, no one would demand that efforts be made to evaluate management development training per se. It is accepted that different models and approaches suit different organisations and individuals. It is hard then to justify such a demand on racism awareness training unless of course institutional racism is in operation to control and contain something which many black trainers understand, but many white trainers find threatening. (Celia Turton of the LGTB, in the report on the CRE seminar on racism awareness training, 1985.)

There may be some strength in the political argument here: considering the limited amount of race relations training that has taken place in this country, the interest in the evaluation of its results has been far greater than would have been expected from the attention previously paid to the evaluation of training in subjects such as health and safety, management techniques and general personnel practices. That disproportionate interest might in some cases come from a suspicion of black professionals 'interfering' in the running of white organisations. However, in other cases it is likely to come from a genuine concern to understand the contribution that training can make towards achieving equality of opportunity, given the very limited success that other measures have so far produced. The main appeal of objective evaluation lies in the hope that it might settle the arguments between competing training principles and methods; often authors claim that particular approaches are the right ones and that other approaches are counter-productive. The arguments are carried out in the literature on the basis of personal training experience or argument from first principles. Little hard evidence of outcomes is brought to bear on the debates.

Racism Awareness Training

The question of the effectiveness of racism awareness training has generated more words than any other single issue in the literature. The argument is plagued with confusions because the term has meant different things to different people at different times. Course titles have picked up the terms 'race awareness', 'racism awareness' and 'racial awareness' with no consistency, and during the period when racism awareness training was a fashionable label it was often attached to any kind of training in the field of race. Recently, however, the indiscriminate use of the term has subsided. Our use of the term should be made clear: the discussion below concerns the training principles and methods based on the 'White Awareness' programme developed by Judy Katz in the USA. The term 'racism awareness training' was taken up by trainers who were incorporating Katz's ideas and material into programmes for tackling racism in this country.

Katz's book *White Awareness: Handbook for anti-racism training* was first published in 1978, and comprised an explanation of the programme's origins and workings and an extensive programme of exercises designed to take white American trainees through a six-stage course. The long-term aims and immediate objectives are best described in Katz's own words:

> The over-all objectives of the program are to help Whites become aware of how racism affects their lives and to help them to change their racist attitudes and behaviours. The program strives to help Whites understand that racism in the United States is a White problem and that being White implies being racist. This understanding is achieved most successfully through (1) confrontation – identifying the discrepancies that exist between what one says and what one does – and (2) a reeducation process – examining history and perspectives through new perceptual filters... If the goals of this program are reached, by the end of the workshop the participants will be able to:
>
> 1. Name and clearly define the concepts of bias, bigotry, prejudice, and racism.
> 2. Describe and examine racism in its institutional, cultural, and individual forms.
> 3. Identify and articulate personal feelings and fears around the issue of racism.
> 4. Define ways in which one's own attitudes and behaviors are representative of racism in the United States.
> 5. Develop and act on specific strategies designed to combat racism on an institutional and individual level.

Katz's emphasis on the discrepancies between what people say and what they do is a corner-stone of her approach. After reviewing 1960s and 1970s research on racism and personality, she extends the analysis of Gunnar Myrdal's 1944 classic study 'An American Dilemma' to the level of individual psychiatry. Myrdal wrote about the contradiction between American constitutional ideals and the racism which is so evident in American history and in its contemporary social order. Myrdal called this a 'deep cultural and psychological conflict'; Katz goes further and argues that it is a disease. It is this pathological approach to racism that leads Katz's programme to place so much emphasis on the individual.

> ...All these analyses clearly indicate that racism is a critical and pervasive form of mental illness... it becomes sadly evident that the psychological disorder racism is deeply embedded in White people from a very early age on both a conscious and unconscious level. The disease has locked them in a psychological prison that victimises and oppresses them every day of their lives.

Katz's course is made up mainly of pair and group exercises that are conducted over several days. The programme is intended to be staffed by one or two facilitators with a 'deep understanding of racism'.

In the early 1980s Katz's book provided an exciting focus for the development of race-related training in Britain. Trainers working mainly in the public sector enthusiastically took up and adapted elements of the programme (Satow, 1982; CRE, 1984; Edmunds and Powell, 1985). One reason for its popularity was its practical accessibility: here, in one volume, was a package of principles, objectives and model exercises. In his critique of the movement, Ahmed Gurnah pointed out that its practicality had a political sense too:

> It appears to address racism not only at the state and institutional level, as do most political activists and academic sociologists, but it is also rightly concerned with people's personal experiences of racism. But in both structural and individual cases, it addresses racism as a practical problem. Particularly after the summer 1981 black rebellions, we cannot over-estimate the appeal of practical solutions to institutional and personal racism. (Gurnah, 1984)

Before long, however, a considerable amount of criticism of racism awareness training emerged, from a number of different directions. First in line were the criticisms from the 'race and class' political stance of the Institute of Race Relations (IRR) which took issue with the basic aims of racism awareness training and saw its development as the latest component of a systematic disabling of the emergent black leadership in the anti-capitalist struggle (Wilson, 1984; Sivanandan 1985). But critiques grounded in more orthodox views of the aims of race relations training started to appear at almost the same time, questioning the psychological and organisational principles of racism awareness training and arguing that its methods did not, after all, offer useful practical solutions to training problems (Gurnah, 1984; Southgate 1984; Banton, 1985; Jervis, 1986).

The IRR developed a precise and well-researched critique of racism awareness training, but it is concerned with the problems of revolutionary socialism, and its arguments are not aimed at the improvement of race relations training; some of the arguments would be equally critical of any other kind of race training, and amount to opposition to the analgesic effect of social reforms that absorb activists into the state apparatus. It is surprising, therefore, that a number of articles subsequently cite Sivanandan's critique as a seminal work in the post-Katz development of race training theory. Gurnah's critique is also political, in the sense that it condemns racism awareness training for diverting energies away from anti-racist action and towards a wallowing in middle-class guilt, but it does acknowledge that training and education are important, and that (some) progress can be made as a result of local authority anti-racist programmes. He also criticises the moral atmosphere of the racism awareness course:

> The tone of RAT is often accusatory and appears to put people on the spot, in order that they may confront themselves. In this sense, it is highly moralistic. Sometimes, what RAT lacks in content, it makes up in highmindedness... The implication is that whites must be made to feel and accept their guilt, whatever else they actually do. This approach is mistaken because individual guilt rarely leads to positive action; and then, it is unclear that even if it did, that it would constitute the right kind of action.

He suggests other negative consequences of racism awareness training: it can arm white officials with the acceptable language of anti-racism and thereby make them free to discriminate unchallenged, and it can unintentionally encourage tokenism. In these respects, it can help the state to cope with black criticisms and manage them more effectively, rather than respond to them genuinely.

The moral tone of racism awareness training is a theme taken up by others. It should be noted that Katz's stated intention was to avoid using guilt as a training tool:

> Unlike many racism awareness programs, this program is not designed to produce guilt or to confront people in a way that 'puts them down.' Guilt often serves to entrench people in their attitudes – to keep them feeling sorry for themselves or others. (Katz, 1978)

In practice, at least some of the training programmes seem to have taken the opposite tack, and critics say that it leads to two problems. Among some trainees, it leads to entrenchment of racist attitudes (as Katz predicted), and, among others, it encourages a perverse lust for guilt and the ritual cleansing of exposure. The popular press have at times been quick to seize on the more lurid stories about racism awareness courses, generally distorting the facts and contributing to a negative image of the whole idea of race training, but there is no doubt that guilt, confrontation and anger have played their part on some of the courses:

> The confrontational aspect of RAT is its most potent weapon. It allows for the unburdening of hidden fears and insecurities – and in the process opens a Pandora's Box of accusation, tears and self-recrimination... Resistance to RAT can be difficult. Silencing techniques, the groundswell of group emotion and the use of emotively tinged sociological terminology thinly defined, effectively cuts out critics who attempt to put forward a broader analysis – criticism can be attributed to defensive prejudice. Thus some participants are forced to leave under a cloud while others go through the process but emerge confused, unable to divorce this from their guilt. Others feel angry and resentful – at one particular session participants were required to wear badges stating 'I am a white racist'. (Jervis, 1986)

Vernon Harris, replying to Jervis, argues that the criticisms of confrontational approaches are based on the white mode of arguing (dispassionate, impersonal, non-challenging, and based on the 'myth of open-mindedness'), and fail to appreciate the black mode (animated, interpersonal, and confrontational). He argues that confrontation reveals the relationship between personal racism and institutional racism:

> The process of confrontation, if successful, makes it exceedingly difficult if not impossible for white people to regard institutional

racism as an extra-human construct, thereby absolving themselves of all responsibility. (Harris, 1987)

Michael Banton (1985) argues to the contrary that racism awareness training fails precisely because it cannot respect 'the boundary between a person's private opinions and that person's competence on the job.' The concept of 'racism', as it is often used now, mixes up prejudice, discrimination and wrong beliefs, and this leads to a misunderstanding of the objectives of training.

Most of the debate about racism awareness training is impressionistic or based on argument from first principles. There is little systematic attempt to assess its successes and failures. Katz's own evaluations were based on pre-course and post-course psychological testing, and showed statistically significant 'improvements' in attitudes. Peter Southgate's study (1984) of courses organised for the police relied on observation by the researcher and reports of the trainees on their experiences; his findings were fairly critical of the exercise, but his conclusions about the future value of racism awareness training were equivocal. From a training perspective, the bulk of the criticisms of racism awareness courses relate to the weakness of the link between the 'conversion' of individuals' attitudes and changes in the way black people are treated by organisations. Although it has generated a lot of heat and noise, racism awareness training has not been seen as very efficient engine of change. It is wrong to see the argument as being simply between trying to change attitudes and trying to change behaviour. None of the advocates of racism awareness training have been concerned with attitudes alone – they have seen behavioural change as the ultimate objective, but have seen attitude change as a vital prerequisite. The real issue is whether racism awareness training can be successful as a first step on the road to reduction of individual and organisational discrimination.

Although the critics of racism awareness training seem to have won the day, recent commentaries have suggested that the more useful elements of the idea have been incorporated in courses with a broader perspective. Rather than reject the whole idea, trainers have inserted some coverage of attitudes and beliefs into courses that focus primarily on the organisation rather than on the individual. Both Tonkin (1987) and Alibhai (1988) argue that this has long been the case, and that 'pure' racism awareness training has been the exception rather than the rule. Evidence of the eclectic approach is to be found within the literature, in accounts of practical experience. For example, Edmunds and Powell (1985) describe the evolution of a multi-racial social work course over the previous five years, and while they acknowledge their debt to Katz's exercises, their approach was open and experimental, pulling in resources from different training traditions. Although they introduced a racism awareness strategy in order to move away from the narrow multi-cultural approach of previous courses, they kept an important multi-cultural component in their course.

> Even in its brief heyday, RAT was never a single entity, but a family group of methods. Applications within SSDs proved to be more eclectic than its critics allow. In practice, RAT and the antiracist training (ART) now favoured by some authorities often share common features, including the stress on the personal dimension of beliefs about race. (Tonkin, 1987)

> In many ways, too, the critics on the left and right have been shooting at an animal that does not exist, wounding others in the process. (Alibhai, 1988)

Practical issues
Splitting issues of theory and principle from issues of practice is in some ways an arbitrary process. However, there are several practical matters which are mentioned in the literature and can usefully be grouped together here to balance the preceding discussion of training principles.

Levels of staff. Which staff in an organisation should receive training related to race? Much of the British literature of practical training applications relates to front-line service delivery (for example, police officers and social workers) or to shop-floor workers and supervisors; in the more general commentaries, however, there is often reference to the need for commitment at higher levels of organisations, where people have more power to change things, and therefore a need for training at managerial grades. Some organisations already have general training programmes which naturally affect a greater proportion of junior staff than they do senior staff; where race training is fitted in with other training it is bound to have a bigger impact on the lower grades, and special measures would need to be taken to draw in more senior staff.

There are indications that training has in practice embraced a growing spectrum of staff levels as the cultural-awareness perspective has given way to an emphasis on racism and discrimination, and as the focus of concern has widened to cover employment as well as service delivery. In all of the examples given in the CRE training guide the training was given at managerial level as well as other levels.

How much is race training informed by other types of training? It is very difficult to tell how far the practical development of training in the race area has been influenced by the theory and practice of other types of training – for example, training in effective management or training for specific professions such as social work. Some of the race training articles and books refer to texts on other areas of training, but the overall impression is that race training either started from scratch in its search for techniques, or absorbed lessons from elsewhere without acknowledging the process.

Integration of race training into other training. The literature shows that race training has in some instances been incorporated into a course or programme that covers other aspects of a persons' job, and in other instances been organised as stand-alone training. There is little discussion over which is preferable, but in terms of the training written about, the balance is in favour of stand-alone courses or programmes.

Training techniques. Between them, Peppard and Shaw provide adequate concepts for describing the range of training techniques used. Didactic methods (conventional teaching involving lectures and note-taking) are counterposed to groupwork methods (group exercises and discussions) and experiential methods (learning from inter-ethnic contacts); conventional teaching and learning from reference material can be called content techniques, while self-discovery exercises, groupwork and experiential learning can be called process techniques.

As race relations training has become more common, the balance has shifted away from conventional teaching and towards process techniques, although it is an open question how much workplace-based race training ever relied solely on formal lectures. The accounts of the development of training in the local authorities and other parts of the public sector show that discussions and exercises form the backbone of training. The design of the exercises and the 'management' of the discussions by trainers is critical to their success: the risk is that trainees merely thrash around in their own prejudices and lack of information, but good exercises and trainers will use them as starting-points for developing a better understanding. In fact the exercises and workshops described in the case studies in the CRE guide show that there is a large 'content' element in the practical implementation of process methods: most sessions have a large substantive input from the trainer or built into the exercise. The same is true for the exercises in the 'White Awareness' programme.

Starting in the trainees' world. Training that goes over people's heads is of no use, whatever the subject. It is clear from the literature that trainers are more successful when their approach is rooted in the professional and social worlds of the trainees. The possibility of a negative, defensive response is minimised by ensuring that the training 'syllabus' and language takes account of (without necessarily accepting) the 'realities' of the job as perceived by the trainees. It is unclear, however, whether trainers who have a deep understanding of the professional tasks involved have an advantage over those who can retain some distance.

Follow-up. The strongest item of consensus in the race training literature is the need for training to be a part of a larger process of change in an organisation. In practice, this does not only mean that courses should be run within the context of an overall equal opportunities programme; it also means that in many cases individual trainees are involved in some kind of follow-up after the course.

3 Equal Opportunities, Business Efficiency and Training

In this chapter we look at the factors influencing the decision of organisations to arrange equal opportunities training, and the relationship between the training and other organisational features and policies.

Different organisations, different approaches

We discussed race relations and equal opportunities training with people working in a very wide range of organisations. What they have in common is their use of some type of course, workshop, briefing session or extended consultancy in order to initiate, facilitate or extend their performance in terms of race equality. Some are private companies while others are in the public sector, and others are charitable bodies; some are large employers with tens of thousands of staff, while others have fewer than twenty; some have well-established arrangements for staff training in other areas of job performance, while others have given little thought to training matters; and some have long histories of interest in equality issues while others are new to the area. Not surprisingly, we found among these different organisations a considerable variety of approaches to equal opportunity training.

An axiom repeated often by trainers and by commentators is that race relations training only makes sense as part of an overall equal opportunities or anti-discrimination programme. In fact the take-up of training without such a programme seems to be rare: in most of the organisations we visited the training has emerged from a general management effort against discrimination, beginning with an equal opportunities policy of some sort. Between organisations there is a great variation in the content of those policies, in the extent of the programmes of action designed to carry them through, and in the motives and initiatives that generated them, but few employers have

31

adopted race relations training without accompanying policies about change. The formal decision to take up training usually comes down from a high level – from executives, board members or elected councillors – but is often filtered through the deliberations of working parties, special staff units devoted to equal opportunities, or individual specialists.

Justice and efficiency

The impetus for change over equal opportunities can come from two different and identifiable directions. One is the moral and political argument about an organisation's responsibility to be fair and to play its part in creating a society free of discrimination and inequality based on race and sex – an argument backed up by the general spirit of the anti-discrimination legislation. The other argument centres on the inefficiency of discrimination and the costs of barring the development of potential within the workforce – particularly now that the supply of young job recruits is beginning to tail off. The 'business sense' argument is also backed by a consideration of the legislation, because employers wish to avoid the inconvenience, bad publicity and costs associated with industrial tribunal cases and CRE formal investigations. Depending on the organisation, one or both of the 'moral' and 'business sense' arguments are deployed to convince decision-makers to adopt the policy; these arguments appear again in the substantive content of training.

It is helpful to remember this dichotomy between justice-oriented approaches and efficiency-oriented approaches. Although bodies and individuals promoting equal opportunities measures tend to use both arguments together to sell the notions of policy change and training, and organisations rarely explain the origins of their own policies purely in terms of one or the other, the approaches are logically distinct. The justice-based arguments would still be valid even if there were no extra benefits in terms of efficiency. In practice, it is clear that some organisations have started from a formal political commitment while others have been strongly influenced by fears of recruitment shortages and doubts about their success in selling to ethnic minority markets. Public sector employers and charitable organisations tend to start from the justice arguments, while private firms tend to cite business reasons for their equal opportunities efforts. In a number of the firms we visited, however, it was the principled commitment of senior staff or board members that started things and kept up the momentum.

> The council came to power with a long equal opportunities manifesto.
> (Local authority training section)

> We were on the hook with the EOC. There was a complaint about our recruitment practices.
> (Large commercial company)

> The current impetus for equal opportunities is the need to respond to the diminishing numbers of young people entering the labour market. We therefore faced pressing business reasons for enhancing the focus on equal opportunities.
> (Large electrical goods manufacturer and supplier)

> The organisation has a written equal opportunities policy which was produced in 1985. The policy was introduced mainly because of the commitment of a new chief executive.
> (Charity with 1,000 staff)

> We've had a policy since 1965. It was paternalistic to begin with, coming from the moral views of the man at the top.
> (Retailing company)

Demand in the public and charitable sectors

It is clear from our interviews with trainers that up to now the majority of paying customers have been in the public sector and the voluntary sector. It is in these sectors that equal opportunities policies have been adopted most frequently and with most vigour on the part of top decision makers. The public sector continues to absorb the attention of many independent trainers, but some commented that with recent changes in local government finance the heyday of public sector training may have passed.

Although many of the public sector bodies that have adopted equal opportunities training are large employers – local authorities and health authorities in particular – there is also a substantial number of smaller public organisations involved, with employees in the hundreds rather than the thousands. In the charitable sector the organisations involved are small, reflecting the general profile of these bodies.

Demand in the private sector

Most of the private-sector firms with a strong equality effort are well known and our research has not extended the list a great deal. A number of large employers with a history of equal opportunities considerations in their employment practices have been joined more recently by others, principally in the financial sector and in the media. Our impression is that the impetus for training on race in the finance sector often comes from a general movement on equal opportunities owing its genesis to concerns over the employment of women; in turn, those concerns have been boosted by an anticipation of the demographic changes which are reducing the pool of potential recruits. Certainly the finance sector has now joined local authorities as one of the sectors where equal opportunities training is relatively common.

Although the visits to companies with race relations training gave us a view of changes in organisations known to have taken equal opportunities measures, they provided little information about what was happening elsewhere. A small survey was therefore conducted by telephone to give some indications of the mood among a more general sample of larger private sector employers. In summary, we can say that the survey revealed very little specific training on race relations, but there seems to be a fairly widespread recognition that good personnel and recruitment practices require a training input and that equal opportunities issues should be one component of it. (See Appendix I for details of the telephone survey of employers.)

The firms in the telephone survey can be divided into several groups, each with a different view of this subject. First, there is a handful of employers where some specific consideration has been given to race and sex equality issues and some training has been arranged around them. Then there is a much larger group, accounting for the majority of firms, which recognise the need for staff to receive some kind of training in recruitment and selection procedures or general personnel management, and make various arrangements to meet that need. Within that group there is a substantial minority (about two fifths of them) who regard race relations or equal opportunities as a component of that general training, although inspection of their detailed replies suggests that most are making an assumption that any training on employment law, recruitment procedures or good employer practices by definition covers equal opportunities. The last group of firms, around one in ten, have no training arrangements in the recruitment or personnel area and see no need for them.

Over a third of all the firms in the sample have some written commitment to equal opportunities (but often a very brief one) and they tend to be the ones claiming to have training in the area. About a quarter of informants from firms without any equality element to their training said that they do have a need for training in this area. Most of those saying that their company has no need for race relations or equal opportunities training regard their current procedures as non-discriminatory and do not see the issue as a problem.

In the private sector the existence of equal opportunities policies and equal opportunities training seems to be strongly related to the size of firms. Nearly all of the companies we visited to discuss their equal opportunities training were found to have over a thousand employees, and the majority employed many thousands. The results of the telephone survey reinforced this picture: written equal opportunity policies existed in over half of the firms with 1,000 or more employees, and in nearly two-thirds of firms with ten or more establishments; by contrast, only 16 per cent of single-site firms had written policies.

Why do organisations seek equal opportunities training?

What do organisations want from race relations and equal opportunities training? Often their aims and objectives are initially unclear, although the demand for training seems to them to be a natural part of organisational change. Indeed some organisations regard training as the first and main element of their programmes. Once they enter a phase of concerted internal discussion, or consultancy with an outside trainer, training aims and objectives tend to become clearer, although this is not always the case.

Our research indicates that, in simple terms, organisations are seeking one or more of the following results from race relations training:

- to get things moving;

- to give a signal that things are moving, particularly to those who are able to put pressure on decision-makers;

- to develop an equality strategy;

- to win over key staff from indifference or opposition to the policy and then persuade and enable them push it forward themselves;

- to deliver technical advice, information and skills that in themselves help the equal opportunities effort of the organisation.

Training to get things moving
For managers, discussions about equal opportunities can seem to lack practical substance, and they have difficulty finding a point at which to initiate action. Training is tangible, and is something of which they have some experience. In some organisations, despite their paper policies, absolutely nothing happens until they begin to think about training. The same effect can be sought in specific parts of an organisation – we heard about training being directed to areas where particular local managers were dragging their feet.

> When the organisation was started in 1980 it was required by its funders to have an EO statement. This was short and vague and nobody thought about EO as a priority in their work. In 1985-6 members of the collective and management committee members went on a racism awareness course... In 1986-7 the EO sub-group was formed and this met every month to work on a collection of policies.
> (Small Voluntary Organisation)

Training to give a signal that things are moving
Training is something visible to staff, executives, board members, council members, and customers. So in terms of employee and public relations, training can be seen as an important symbolic first step.

> Training was not strictly mandatory, but you would not be allowed to interview without training. The members wanted to demonstrate that they were serious about the policy.
> (Local authority)

Training to develop an equality strategy
This is a specific objective that some organisations use trainers to help them pursue. A typical format would be one or a series of information sessions and workshops for senior staff or policy makers during which the race relations or equal opportunities policy and programme is planned, examined or built up.

> We felt the course should be seen as part of organisation development... The course was also concerned with clarifying the organisation's position with regard to the racial dimension of the service we provide.
> (Voluntary organisation)

Training to win over key staff

The idea behind this kind of training is that spreading responsibility for the policy down through the organisation should make it self-sustaining. 'Key staff' here means different things in different organisations: in some cases it extends only as far as senior personnel managers, while in others line-managers throughout the organisation are included.

> All managers involved with recruitment were trained nationwide, and all people involved in personnel... The aim is to get everyone conversant with their responsibilities and to get branch managers to see equal opportunities as part of their business objectives.
> (Large financial company)

Training to deliver technical advice, information and skills

Examples are an understanding of the race relations legislation and standardised fair interviewing techniques for recruitment and selection.

> The people being trained are those who interview on the milk-round and others... The whole thrust of recruitment and selection programmes is that they should be free from recruiter bias and interviewee reaction...
> (Minerals company)

Who takes the decisions?

In most organisations, irrespective of sector, the decision to adopt training as part of the equal opportunities effort is taken along with the decisions on overall moves on equality – in other words, equal opportunities training usually owes its existence to its inclusion in the original package of measures. Usually the overall equal opportunities policy is established at a high level of an organisation; it could be said, therefore, that the decisions over equal opportunities training are taken at the level of senior management, board or council. However, the real practical choices about training are mostly taken at lower levels, for two reasons. First, the high-level decisions tend to be based on plans proposed by others, such as personnel and human resources managers, departmental management, special working parties or outside consultants; and, secondly, the high-level sanctioning of equal opportunities training tends to be a simple agreement in principle, leaving the more detailed decisions about the type of training and the trainers to more junior managers.

In the private sector, the equal opportunities training is usually organised by a manager in the training or personnel department. Some firms, however, have appointed an equal opportunities manager, who is often then given responsibility for training in this area. Because of the tie-up between equal opportunities issues and personnel management, there is a need for close collaboration between managers on the training side and those working in personnel; in the organisations we visited, there seem to be good working relationships between the different areas of responsibility, at least as far as equal opportunities training is concerned. The arrangements are simpler in companies where general training is centralised; in companies where the training responsibilities are partly devolved to departments, to geographical regions or to profit centres, the equal opportunities training tends to be centrally encouraged and organised, but the progress can be uneven and in some cases the component organisations make their own arrangements. Some very large firms have a training section that effectively sells training to other divisions (or other companies within a group), and the spread of equal opportunities training relies heavily on encouragement at board level.

General managerial and personnel arrangements also vary between companies with different levels of centralisation and corporate control, although the implications for equal opportunities efforts in each case are difficult to predict. In some companies the unchallengeable, centrally-issued instruction to subsidiaries or branches is a powerful tool, and once a particular practical component of the equal opportunities programme is agreed at the centre it can be implemented rapidly. In our discussions with employers we found large companies where progress on equality relied partly on this procedure, to great effect. But bureaucratic control of managerial and personnel practice can also slow things down, and in other centralised firms we found frustration resulting from the inertia of an organisation that seemed too big to change at any speed. Similarly, in the large groups with decision-making power devolved to individual businesses there is no straightforward implication for equal opportunities: within each component businesses a good equality programme has more scope to influence mainstream managerial practices and structure, but those businesses are also free to ignore the issue altogether. We found uneven progress within these decentralised groups, both on equal opportunities generally and on race-related training in particular, with good headway made in some organisations but none in others in the same group. Some groups make an effort to give central guidance on equal opportunities as part of corporate culture, producing training materials and employing equality officers at head office, but there does seem to be a real difference of style and impact between the issuing of instructions to component businesses and simply making facilities available to use they want them. Unless equality of opportunity is made a corporate objective, it is easily overshadowed at a local level in the struggle to meet the main business objectives, because it is seen as something that has a local cost but no short-term local benefit. If its benefit is felt largely in the long-term, then it needs to be promoted as part of group strategy, and is therefore best encouraged from the centre as a business objective in its own right.

In local authorities the situation is parallel to that in the private sector, in that the responsibility is spread between managers in personnel, general training and equal opportunities, although managers and units with special responsibility for equal opportunities are more common in this sector. High-level decisions about equal opportunities tend to have a more detailed content than in the private sector – race relations is the subject of manifesto commitments and local politics, and members sitting on council committees exercise a considerable degree of direct control over the substance of policy. Also, the implementation of policy in this area is a much more public affair than it is in the private sector; decisions to adopt one programme of training or another can come under the scrutiny of electors, pressure groups and the media.

In the charitable and voluntary sector the decisions over equal opportunities matters, including training, tend to be taken at directorial or management council level, but also involve consultation and negotiation with other staff members and staff groups. There is a size effect here, because smaller organisations do not have so many layers of decision-making as larger ones, but there is also a difference in style of operation: charitable and voluntary bodies often aspire to a democratic and participative management style, hence the apparently greater degree of staff and member consultation. Nevertheless, in some large charitable organisations the practical decisions about training are mainly in the hands of personnel and training managers.

The importance of general training arrangements

Nearly all of the organisations with equal opportunities training had substantial programmes of general training for their staff. Most of the organisations are large and have their own central or departmental training sections; in the smaller organisations there are less elaborate training structures, but they do tend to have explicit staff training strategies with ear-marked budgets.

Organisations utilise their existing training arrangements to introduce race relations and equal opportunities training to varying degrees. Some integrate the new training into courses already running, by adding equal opportunities sessions. Others set up new courses within the existing training framework, or replace old courses. In all cases, however, it appears that the existence of a ready-made structure plays an important part in facilitating the introduction of equality work. We have to conclude that organisations with little or no training in management and personnel matters are unlikely to develop any equal opportunities training; in support of this, the results of the telephone survey show that none of the firms without training arrangements for personnel matters claimed to have arranged any equal opportunities training. This is related to the tendency of training to be the first concrete measure in an equal opportunities programme: if an organisation has a training infrastructure, and staff are accustomed to the idea of innovation and career development through training, then training is likely to be seen as a powerful tool, ready to hand, for implementing equality policies. Other measures, such as changes of mainstream employment or customer relations policies, ethnic record keeping and monitoring, targeting or positive action, require new structures and new thinking.

Organisational change and individual duties

One of the more sterile debates about training has concerned the relative merits of pursuing equality through changes in individual attitudes, through changes in individual behaviour, and through shifts in organisational policy and practice. Our visits to employers showed that under the banner of race relations and equal opportunities training people seek in different circumstances to do one or both of the following: to facilitate policy change for overall improvement in an organisation's equality performance or to equip individual staff to do their jobs better, to the same end. The best choice seems to depend on the type of organisation and the stage of development of its equality effort, and not on an across-the-board judgement of the 'correct' way to do race training. The formal aspects of the organisation's functioning needs to be considered – for example, a public service and a manufacturing plant require different approaches to equal opportunities – and there is a need for a sensitive appreciation of the organisational culture, which can at one and the same time be an impediment to progress and a necessary starting point for change.

As described earlier, training as an input to organisational change often involves courses and workshops for decision makers at a fairly high level – sometimes senior staff, and sometimes members of boards or councils. The overall functioning of the organisation and the equality implications of policy are on the agenda in these sessions. It is notable that among the organisations we visited, the voluntary and charitable bodies have more commonly than others started with training aimed at substantial organisational overhaul, possibly because they are usually relatively small, and possibly because their moves towards equal opportunity programmes are often based on political pressure or moral questioning and therefore tend to be more searching from their inception.

The natural history of equal opportunities training within an organisation tends to run from the general to the specific, and from the top downwards: that is to say initial training efforts concern awareness or general concepts of equal opportunity, and concentrate on senior staff or middle-grade staff, while later on training concerns more practical issues such as recruitment and selection, provided for staff at lower levels. This is only a general trend, with notable exceptions, and it is true of large organisations more often than of small ones; it is also mixed up with the wider history of race training in this country, which has over the last ten years moved into and out of a phase of emphasis on 'awareness', and towards an emphasis on the functioning of the organisation. In the local authority sector this has been characterised by the change in course titles from 'racism awareness training' to 'anti-racism training'.

In all sectors the training arranged for individual staff members comprises a mixture of duty-oriented and discretion-oriented content, the balance between the two often depending on the nature of the organisation and the nature of the job in question. Duty-oriented elements involve explanations of rules, legal obligations and formal duties. Discretion-oriented elements involve attempts to dispel misinformed beliefs and encourage a better understanding of the ways in which racism and discrimination seep into the performance of a job. Jobs differ in the extent to which they are governed by formal rules and by personal judgement, and it is unrealistic to expect improvements in their equality performance to be accessible with a uniform approach.

4 Provision of Race Related Training

Race relations training in Britain has been provided through a number of different channels, all of which were included in the round of interviews for this study. They can be grouped as follows:

- *(i) Publicly-funded services*
  - Race Relations Employment Advisory Service
  - Industrial Language Training Units
  - Commission for Racial Equality
  - Race Equality Councils
  - Other publicly funded training services
- *(ii) Independents*
  - Independent training consultancies
  - – commercial
  - – non-profit
  - Independent freelance trainers
- *(iii) Associations*
  - Public sector employers' organisations
  - Professional associations
- *(iv) Labour movement*
  - TUC
  - Individual trade unions
- *(v) In-house*
  - Organisations' own internal training sections

(i) Publicly funded services
The Department of Employment's Race Relations Employment Advisory Service provides employers with free advice and training. About twenty-five advisers operate nationwide from a number of locations around the country, each reporting to one of the two regional administrative centres in London and Sheffield. The service aims to make about 1,000 visits to employers (including repeat visits) and provides 800 to 900 briefing seminars per year.

The Industrial Language Training Units were in the past an important element of race training provision in this country, and some were still functioning at the time of our fieldwork, but they no longer exist as a national network of Units. The Manpower Services Commission published an extensive review of the ILT Service in 1985, and subsequently the Units ceased to receive dedicated government funding. Some Local Education Authorities absorbed former ILTU staff and in these areas training provision continues on a reduced scale.

The staff of the Commission for Racial Equality advise employers about their obligations under the Race Relations Act and carry out general promotional work on equal opportunities. They provide a small amount of training for employers and trade unions, and arrange seminars and conferences on equal opportunities employment and on race training itself. Race Equality Councils (formerly Community Relations Councils) arrange local meetings and seminars and some open courses on race equality in employment and service delivery; the extent of their involvement in this kind of work varies considerably from place to place.

There is a small number of other publicly-funded providers of race relations training. They are for the most part in receipt of grants for supplying training to specific sectors such as the police or voluntary organisations.

(ii) Independent trainers and consultancies

The PSI project has concentrated on London, the Midlands and West Yorkshire. Within those areas there are several dozen 'independents'. These are either training consultancies (organised as commercial firms or as non-profit services) or freelance individuals, offering race relations training or equal opportunities training that covers race among other subjects. The supply side of the market changes quite rapidly, but we estimate that in the study areas a 'yellow pages' of race relations training would include about 50 to 60 entries for the independents.

It is important to note that among the independent providers are organisations and individuals with very diverse histories in race training. Some have come into the business through their work in management training and organisational development, while the involvement of others has grown out of their experience in campaigning for the rights of black people and other groups. Some of the independents specialise in race training while others provide it as part of a longer menu of training services. Some are businesses which aim to turn a commercial profit, while others aim to make only enough money to continue their work. Whatever the background of the trainers, however, we have observed among them a generally high level of commitment to race and sex equality and to the role of training in achieving it. Some continue to work in the field at a cost of personal stress, because the training is often emotionally demanding: even when trainers avoid 'confrontational' methods, participants often find the subject very uncomfortable and in response try to undermine the trainer, sometimes behaving abusively, particularly towards black trainers and women trainers. As a result, we were told, there is some tendency for people to 'burn out' professionally after a few years, as in other stressful occupations.

(iii) Associations
Although their role is often one of promotion and co-ordination rather than direct provision of training, some public sector employers' organisations help to arrange race relations training for their constituent bodies. Some professional associations and institutes are also keen promoters of training and include race relations on their general syllabuses.

(iv) Labour movement
The TUC includes an element on racism and discrimination in its basic courses for shop stewards and staff representatives. The ten-day courses, within which race relations takes up one day, are run through the TUC's regional structure; in the South East region, for example, the courses are run from thirty different centres. There are also three and five day courses on 'Tackling Racism at Work' run at the TUC National Education Centre and at a number of TUC sponsored local centres. Individual trade unions have raised their profile on equal opportunities issues over the last few years, and several now run special race relations courses for lay members and full-time officers.

(v) In-house training
Many large organisations have their own general staff training schemes, often administered by corporate or departmental training sections, and some have taken on race relations as part of their work.

This is particularly evident in the local authority sector, where in some cases staff have been appointed specially to organise equal opportunities training. Also common is the 'topping-up' of in-house training programmes by the use of outside trainers. This happens in two distinct ways: first by the supplementing of 'bulk' training by the addition of race relations and other equal opportunities modules; and secondly by the use of outsiders to instruct in-house trainers, who in turn carry out the main programme within the organisation.

As large organisations move through different stages of equal opportunities development and attempt to give training to staff in greater numbers and at lower levels, so buying in training becomes economically less efficient than running a programme with their own trainers. The training of in-house trainers seems to be a growing part of the equal opportunities scene. A number of the independents mentioned this aspect of their work, some of them claiming to be the only pioneers in field – probably because the work is relatively new and there has not been a significant discussion of it in the literature.

Training courses on the market

It is a good idea to distinguish between two types of course:
(i) Courses for staff of a single organisation, tailored to that organisation.
(ii) Courses open to people from more than one organisation.

(i) Courses tailored to a single organisation

Most of the trainers (both publicly-funded and independent) offer these courses, which make up the bulk of the training discussed in our interviews. The degree of tailoring varies a great deal. It is rare that an organisation will buy in a course that takes no account of their particular circumstances and problems, but sometimes trainers make only minor amendments to courses they ran previously.

The variety hidden behind the term 'courses' should not be underestimated. They range from short information sessions on the law and the concept of indirect discrimination through to programmes of workshops stretching over many months and involving organisational development, personal development and training for skills, knowledge and beliefs; from seminars for senior managers through to instruction sessions on job duties for manual staff; from courses on personnel practice through to courses on equality in service delivery. Within this diversity it is very hard to judge where the centre of gravity lies – that is to say in what form the largest volume of race relations training has taken place – but our work suggests that courses in fair recruitment and selection take precedence, followed by courses or workshops on equality of service delivery. Recruitment and selection training tends to be used by employers as a formal way of introducing equal opportunities development to their workforce.

The most common length of the discrete courses on recruitment and selection, or on awareness, is two to three days, although one-day courses are not uncommon. Many trainers prefer to run longer courses because they feel they are more effective, and for obvious commercial reasons, and some employers take up courses of five days. Courses extending beyond a week are rare, although some of those we heard about were broken up into sections over several months adding to more than a week in total. Most outside trainers have a preference for running courses away from the employer's premises, partly for practical reasons, to avoid trainees being called away to the telephone or to attend to crises, and partly to assist trainees in thinking in new ways about their work. These two reasons are not as distinct as they might seem at first: reluctant trainees tend to use a work crisis as an excuse to duck out of challenging parts of a course, and it was suggested to us that people even arrange for radio-page bleeps to sound at convenient times. Off-site training is not always practicable, however, and in many cases has the disadvantage of adding to the cost of a course.

(ii) Open courses

A number of bodies run publicly advertised open courses and seminars on race relations and equal opportunities issues (for example the Industrial Society, the Royal Institute of Public Administration (RIPA), the CRE, and some of the independents). While open courses do not possess the same scope for diversity as courses within organisations, they do vary a good deal, between concerns with employment and service delivery, between different sectors, and over the extent to which they emphasise the role of the individual in establishing equality practices.

Training and equal opportunities consultancy

Most of the providers (both the independents and the publicly-funded trainers) feel that it is important to combine their equal opportunities training with other organisational development work and other staff development work. Nearly all trainers hold the view that training can only be part of a general strategy to improve the equality performance of an employer or a service, and they seek to contribute in other ways to that strategy. In many cases the course planning merges into a phase of general equal opportunities consultancy; most trainers are not only interested in the extra work, but are also committed to a successful equal opportunities outcome. They do not want the training to be an isolated event. Sometimes clients have to be talked out of regarding training as their main (or in extreme cases their only) equal opportunities measure.

Course design and assessing training needs

The starting point of both training and consultancy is the 'needs assessment', much discussed in the literature but in practice a stage that is often reduced to a discussion and exchange of information between a trainer and a manager in the client organisation. Trainers differ in what they offer, however, and what clients expect to happen also varies, so it is worth outlining the range of preliminary assessments of training requirements that were described in our interviews.

In principle most trainers like to spend some time studying an organisation, to identify the specific problems and options, before recommending a training course and other measures. The aims are to identify particular impediments to equality in the formal and informal functioning of the organisation, and the points at which discrimination can occur by design or by default, and to determine which of these are accessible by training and which can be tackled by other policies; one trainer said the point is to 'get under the skin' of an organisation. In some cases this assessment is possible, where an employer accepts the value of the exercise (and the implied challenge to managerial prerogative) and resources are available to fund the work. The publicly-funded training services have to convince employers of the first point, but do not have to persuade them to pay the full cost, so they have in general undertaken more substantial needs assessment exercises than the independents, who need to recoup the full cost from the client. Trainers explained to us that most organisations do not have the level of commitment required to put money 'up front' for equal opportunities and that firms in the private sector are particularly reluctant. Some trainers insist, however, on a minimum consultation before training, and some are successful in mounting substantial needs assessment exercises within companies, involving discussions with managers, staff and customers over a period of weeks. Market position is of some importance here: trainers in greater demand and with a firmer reputation seem to be in a better position to convince employers of the value of preliminary research and consultation, while others report that they usually have to compromise. All resist going in cold without any consultation.

Typically, trainers have an initial meeting with a representative of the client, usually a manager or personnel officer, to discuss the basic objectives of the training and possible approaches, and for the trainer to learn about the organisation. The trainer will probably take away written materials on the structure, functioning and history of the organisation and the department or section where the training is to take place. Another meeting will take place after a more detailed training plan has been developed, and there might be one or two other meetings with key managers or staff; in rare cases the trainers meet all the trainees in advance. In this way an agreed course is worked out. Although this process is better described as tailoring courses to organisations than as comprehensive assessment of needs, it is often the case that clients are persuaded to drop the training they originally had in mind and to adopt another course instead.

It is worth noting that even the minimal pre-course tailoring is not practicable on the open courses, which take trainees from a number of organisations. Some open courses are aimed at particular sectors and particular types of occupation, but they cannot account in advance for the specific organisational setting in the same way as a course designed for a particular workplace.

Costs
(i) Courses and consultancy within an organisation
RREAS make no charges for their services. The CRE and the RECs have no fixed charging policy and often carry out training for nominal fees. When the ILT Service was operational, its charges varied between Units and between clients.

Most of the independents explained that they charge a daily rate per trainer. Many said that the actual rate is negotiable and depends on the type of client: profit-making organisations are charged higher rates than public sector organisations, which in turn pay more than charities, community-based organisations and campaigning bodies. It should be noted that there is more than one argument behind this scaling of charges. One is that some non-profit organisations have little money, and without a discount they simply would not be able to afford the training; another is that private sector organisations can afford more than public sector organisations (one might question whether that assumption holds invariably). A proportion of trainers are also politically more sympathetic to the equal opportunities efforts of public-sector and voluntary organisations than they are to the efforts of firms in the private sector. Some trainers work only in the public and voluntary sectors by choice; others find themselves in the same position because of the smaller take-up of race relations training in the private sector.

For the majority of trainers, daily rates per trainer in the public sector were in 1988 between £200 and £300; a small number, however, started at £500 or more per trainer. The top (commercial) end of the scale was, for the majority of trainers, less than £600 per day. This means that an 'average' course using two trainers and lasting three days could have cost anywhere between £1,200 and £3,600 – but would most often be around £1,500 to £2,000. The additional costs of pre-course consultancy and needs assessment are harder to establish, because trainers are more vague about them, but the pattern seems to be for a lower charge rate for pre-course work. This is perhaps because it is less in demand – clients usually try to avoid buying much time other than actual training days. Although trainers stress the importance of preparatory work, many employers seem to be unconvinced and prefer to spend their money on what they see as a more tangible product. For this reason, and because the client's demands vary considerably with the size of the organisation, it is impossible to give a figure for an average package of consultancy plus training.

Several informants said that they had on occasions provided training for no charge for organisations that were particularly deserving and poor, and when seeking to open up new areas of business.

(ii) Open courses
For these there is a charge per trainee, and again there is a wide range, from under £40 per day to over £150 per day (1988 prices).

The implications of different funding arrangements
The way in which trainers are funded is one of the influences on their patterns of work and their approaches to 'training principles'. The fact that organisations are comparatively reluctant to pay for extensive consultancy in the run-up to training means that publicly funded and grant funded trainers (such as RREAS and the ILTUs, but also other trainers who have institutional backing) have had greater flexibility than independent trainers in dealing with clients. Background funding permits a greater input of non-training hours. Thus trainers with background funding tend to carry out more overall equal opportunities consultancy as a pre-requisite to training, and more extensive follow-up. In this way, funding does affect the type of training a client receives.

The involvement of institutions
There is no professional body or other organisation that keeps an up-to-date comprehensive register of race relations training providers. Consequently people who are seeking training have to rely on a variety of formal and informal sources of information. Useful advice has been disseminated by the CRE in its two-volume guide to race relations training, and other bodies have given direct or indirect encouragement to employers to take up training, but none have provided the tools to begin a proper search for trainers. The Local Government Training Board produced a non-evaluative register of trainers, but it is now out of date. The National Health Service Training Authority produced a register of trainers more recently. However, the most common starting point for organisations seems to be a set of enquiries among professional contacts.

People starting their search for a provider of race relations training sometimes contact the CRE, PSI or another national organisation associated in some way with race relations. The present arrangements (or, rather, lack of arrangements) for providing lists of potential trainers cannot be fair or efficient. The institutions involved with race relations ought arguably to take on an explicit role in this respect, because de facto they already have one, like it or not. Potential clients also have difficulties in establishing criteria for selecting trainers, and need to be advised of what questions to ask, not just of the trainers, but of themselves: sometimes organisations do not have a clear idea about what they want from training before they embark on a selection process.

Networks and individuals

It would be wrong to visualise the independent sector of training provision as being made up of consultancies, with permanent full-time staff, operating independently of and in competition with individual freelance trainers. The reality is much more complicated, and is better characterised as a set of partially interlocking networks rather than a field of discrete competitors. This is not to deny that there are professional rivalries as in any other business, nor to suggest that all freelance trainers have connections with others; there is in fact a robust atmosphere of competitive professional pride among trainers (fed by the very public debates over training principles) but it co-exists with a degree of functional collaboration. The consultancies tend to employ people who at other times do freelance work or who have permanent part-time jobs elsewhere. 'Training associate' was a term used repeatedly in our interviews, referring to trainers who work together on a semi-permanent basis or who can be brought in for specific courses or sessions. Arrangements like these mean that the commercial and employment structures of training provision are more fluid than they might at first appear, especially as professional collaborations and alliances tend to shift over time. Freelance trainers who do not have professional links with others complain of isolation, however, since there are no formal professional structures. Periodically there are attempts to establish more formal networks and forums for equal opportunities trainers, but these have not developed enough momentum – or resources – to overcome the barriers created by the 'training debate', and trainers still seek to differentiate themselves publicly in terms of training principle and commitment to race equality.

Marketing

As regards marketing their product, the consensus among the independent trainers is that standard advertising methods (such as newspapers and magazines) have little effect. Most business comes by recommendation or by repeat orders. Some commented that mail shots to potential customers do generate some work, and some business comes from telephoning likely clients.

Selecting trainers

Finding an outside trainer is at present largely a matter of asking professional contacts or consulting trainers already known. Most of the clients we have spoken to found their trainers through informal contacts of this sort. Over half, however, considered more than one provider before taking them on. Several, in both the public sector and the private sector, adopted a fairly formal procedure for selection from the group of trainers they contacted, although we have seen little evidence of selection of trainers by simple competitive tender. Organisations do pick and choose, but more often through a process of discussion with trainers over what they will provide than through a crude assessment of value for money. Some organisations now scrutinise trainers on an on-going basis and maintain an approved list, from which trainers are taken on for specific tasks.

Client informants made few comments about the importance of costs for their choice of trainer. In the end, for large organisations at least, race relations training at a senior staff level is not an expensive purchase: two to three thousand pounds for three days' intensive training for over a dozen professional staff is relatively good value, and employers can therefore afford to choose the course they want on the basis of perceived quality rather than price. In the private sector, our client informants suggested that the financial arguments about equal opportunities training centred on its contribution to saving money later, rather than worries about its cost; the training has to be justified in terms of its contribution to better uses of human resources, better marketing, or, in some cases, avoidance of the expense of industrial tribunals and formal investigations. This is not to say that costs are irrelevant: some commented that one factor that made RREAS attractive was the fact that their services are free. Independent trainers complained that clients often want training (like any other product or service) for low costs, and some clients even assume at first that it is always free.

Several of the consumers have experience of more than one outside training provider. Some work with more than one simultaneously, while others have changed because they required a different sort of training, or because they were unhappy with the work of the previous provider.

The training effort

The content of the training we heard about in the interviews is extremely varied, as is the degree of integration into mainstream training. Although we tend to talk about 'courses' as if they are always discrete events, the race relations training is sometimes embedded in training programmes with a wider coverage, even if it is handled with the assistance of trainers brought in specially.

In the organisations we visited, the main areas of concern of the courses have been: general equal opportunities concepts and strategies of change; awareness of racism and discrimination; fair recruitment and selection; personnel policy and practice; ethnic monitoring principles and procedures; and equality in public service delivery. Most of the courses have been a mixture of several of these elements, although some are run as single-subject courses – for example, recruitment and selection courses. Common to most courses, irrespective of their other content, is an attempt to give people a conceptual framework and language to deal with the ideas of racism, discrimination and equality of opportunity – to clear the ambiguities and prejudices about these terms. Without this, the lack of a common language and a clear set of terms describing the different causes of inequality leads to misunderstandings, which prevent the discussion of equal opportunities developing very far.

Most of the race relations training on employment issues has been among managers, supervisors and personnel staff. Training with a service delivery emphasis has more often also taken in staff with other responsibilities, including 'front line' staff such as social workers and counter staff. Most courses mix grades of staff, although trainers are wary of the breadth of grades being too wide, for several reasons. First, the aims and design of a course will depend on the jobs of the participants, and it is confusing and unproductive to try to cover too many functions in an organisation at once; secondly, trainees need to have some common experience for the group tasks and discussions to work properly; and thirdly, senior staff can intimidate others, with or without intent, if the gap is too wide.

In-house training staff are commonly given race relations training, either to ensure that the equal opportunities stance of the organisation is reflected in (or at least not contradicted by) the style and substance of mainstream training, or to leave them equipped to take over from outside trainers and continue the programme of race relations training. Passing on the baton from outside trainers to in-house trainers is more common among the larger employers, including local authorities, where buying in training in bulk would be very expensive.

What is available?

One important concern of organisations seeking race relations or equal opportunity training is the actual content of the courses available from outside trainers. At this point it is vital that we do not ask the wrong questions: one unfortunate legacy of the racism awareness debate is that people tend to look at race relations training as if it were a single entity, one that some courses do successfully and others do unsuccessfully. But the array of available courses for race relations training does not represent a plethora of different approaches to the same objective, from which we need to choose the ones that work and reject those that fail; rather, it reflects the variety of aims which training is employed to pursue. Any answer to the question 'what is the best way of going about race relations training?' is bound to be unsatisfactory because 'race relations training' is a term that embraces many activities, all of which are useful in specific circumstances but not in others. This is perhaps the most important way in which much of the literature on equal opportunities training has failed to reflect what actually happens in the field.

The market offers training to meet many different needs: management of organisational change, awareness of the needs of ethnic minority clients, equality pitfalls in interviewing and selection, details of the Race Relations Act and other legislation, general equal opportunities action programmes, and many other aspects of equality and race relations, designed for trainees at many different levels in organisations that are at different stages of policy development. Trainers tend to offer a range of services but also have their own specialisms. Therefore once an organisation is sure of what its training aims are, there should be few difficult issues to resolve in selecting training providers – few, that is to say, exclusive to this subject area. It is in the assessment of the aims that the difficulties lie: in other words, you can probably find the training your organisation needs, but you might first have to work to identify that need.

Trainers differ in the extent to which they stress the distinctiveness of race equality as opposed to other equality issues. Some feel that treating race discrimination as just one example of discrimination against oppressed groups is the best way to start people thinking about racism. They argue that trainees are better able to accept the general principles behind measures to ensure equality when the case is broadly put. Pointing out together the discrimination against people with disabilities, against women and against minority ethnic groups overcomes the defensiveness about race often felt by white trainees and helps them avoid feelings that black people are being preferred by 'reverse discrimination'. This is a practical argument for dealing with all the 'isms' together; others say that the broad equal opportunities approach is also better in principle, because equality-centred thinking should be comprehensive in its approach to disadvantaged groups, and that there is little point in overhauling an organisation's policy and practice towards one group then moving on to another. Others argue to the contrary that covering race issues in a general course on equality cannot succeed unless the special nature of racism is addressed; that is not to say that other forms of discrimination are less important, but that racism cannot be understood by simple analogy to discrimination against women and disabled people. They argue that dealing with racial discrimination as one of several pitfalls of inequality leaves unfinished business – particularly with regard to the trainees' own feelings on the matter.

Content of typical courses

Having stressed the variety of training available, we should point out that for each training objective there is a surprising degree of convergence of course content. Trainers may argue about principles, but these generally affect choices of aims and objectives, and they are less divided over what should go into, say, an actual course on bias-free interviewing, or a policy development workshop for senior managers. To illustrate this, a typical programme is shown below for each of three types of training: recruitment and selection, company equal opportunities policy, and general anti-discrimination and equal opportunity practices for service providers. As a rule, less attention should be paid to course titles than to their stated programmes, since titles are prone to vary with fashion and even with differing regional acceptability of terms such as 'anti-racism': one trainer told us that course titles were consciously toned down outside the capital to account for this.

Example Programme 1: Recruitment and Selection

This is a course for line managers with responsibility for recruitment and promotion, held within an organisation that has an equal opportunity policy and programme. The aim is to make the policy clear in respect of recruitment and selection, to give trainees an understanding of the problems of direct and indirect discrimination, and to give them guidelines for ensuring their own practices are fair and seen to be fair.

(Two Day Programme)

1. Equality Policy and Procedure -
   The company equality programme. (Introduction and discussion).

2. Indirect Discrimination -
   How selection procedures affect people's chances. (Group exercise and discussion).

3. Fair Recruitment Procedures -
   Preparing job descriptions and person specifications. (Small group exercises and discussion).

4. Fair Selection Part 1 -
   Shortlisting. (Group exercise).

5. Fair Selection Part 2 -
   Interviewing skills. (Group exercise, small group exercise, and role play).

6. Summary -
   Review of course. (Small group reports and discussion).

Example Programme 2: Company Equal Opportunity Policy

This is an in-house introductory course for all managerial and personnel staff in a company with an established equal opportunity policy with ethnic record keeping, monitoring and targets. It is part of junior management training and the induction of senior managers new to the company. The aims are to make clear the company commitment to equal opportunities and to demonstrate its practical implications.

(One Day Programme)

1. Discrimination and the Law -
    The Sex Discrimination Act and the Race Relations Act. (Lecture and discussion).

2. Company Policy -
    Implications of the law for the company. The Codes of Practice. (Group exercise and discussion).

3. Good and Bad Practice -
    Operating the policy. (Small group exercises).

4. Meeting Goals and Targets-
    Equal opportunities as part of the company's corporate planning. (Group and individual exercises).

Example Programme 3: Anti-discrimination and Equal Opportunity Practices for Service Provision

This is an open course for people working in public, voluntary and charitable service provision. The aims are to introduce the concepts of racism, discrimination and mono-culturalism, showing how they can affect the delivery of services and the staffing of organisations, and to suggest ways that organisations can change.

(One Day Programme)

1. Introduction -
    Trainees' expectations and concerns. (Individual exercise and group discussion).

2. The Influence of Culture -
    Awareness of the influence of cultural assumptions on trainees' behaviour. (Small group exercises).

3. Defining Terms -
    What is racism? What is discrimination? (Group exercise and discussion).

4. Example: Racial Disadvantage in Employment -
    How does it come about? (Small group exercises and discussion).

5. Equal Opportunities in Action -
   Ways of avoiding discrimination and fighting racism
   in practice. Equal opportunities policies. (Small
   group exercises and discussion).

Training methods

Most race relations and equal opportunities training is now based on
a mixture of methods, with an emphasis on the value of group work
and self-discovery. This is in line with a general trend in staff training
methods, irrespective of the subject matter. Courses tend to be based
on groups of eight to fifteen trainees, most commonly with two
trainers. Workshops and discussions are used extensively, and the
didactic chalk-and-talk methods are out of fashion. The newer
methods do not make a course into a non-directed free-for-all, because
they are strategically designed to bring trainees to desired conclusions
and move them through the course syllabus. The degree of guidance
varies and, depending on the skills of the trainer, the trainees' arrival
at successive stages of the learning process can seem natural or it can
be something of a battle. However, the dependence of group training
methods on the skills and experience of the trainer is not special to
race and equal opportunities training.

Different courses are run for different levels of staff. This is true
for the form of training as well as the substance. Just as the more senior
staff tend to have broader, more policy-oriented training than others,
so they also tend to receive it in less formal ways: seminar-type work
is more common at this level than it is for intermediate and junior staff.
No courses at any level are predominantly lecture-based.

Many of the trainers use video films to trigger some of the
discussions, but they play down the importance of the content of
particular videos. The films are used for keeping up the momentum
of courses and introducing ideas in a different way. One trainer said
he was keen to ensure that videos amplify points already under
discussion, and do not 'slip into mere entertainment'. Consumers of
equal opportunities training seem to give a higher value to videos,
however. We were often told by training managers, personnel
managers and equal opportunities managers that particular videos had
a profound effect on trainees' personal understanding of prejudice and
discrimination. The trainers we spoke to mentioned a wide variety of
videos: some are special training films, while others are recordings of

relevant television programmes. Some of the training films are commercially available while others are produced by the trainers themselves. Some employers produce their own audio-visual materials for internal use.

Some of the equal opportunities training in large organisations, particularly in the finance sector, is currently provided by distance-learning methods (videos, computer-based learning packages, and interactive videos) which are commonly used for their general staff training programmes. It remains to be seen how far these methods will be taken up elsewhere, and how effective they are, either as a component of a wider equal opportunities training strategy or as the main form of an organisation's training.

Collections of written training materials are built up by individual trainers and agencies, who tend to be constantly looking out for new exercises, examples and case-studies. Written materials are often developed from the trainers' experiences in their client organisations: each organisation brings up new equal opportunities problems, which can be used anonymously as practical case studies for future courses. Several trainers said that these examples from personal experience are much more useful than material borrowed from other trainers or taken from training books, although some said they do compare and share materials.

As in the case of the videos, trainers play down the importance of the substantive content of written material, saying that they are just props to facilitate processes that are essentially interpersonal. This relaxed approach to the importance of the content does, however, seem to conflict with a reluctance of some trainers to reveal their materials, and frequent references to people pirating others' materials. But their proprietary concerns over materials are also founded on a genuine worry about the misuse of their tools, for there is a fear among trainers that some of their clients (or potential clients) would, if they had access to the materials, try to take on the training themselves, without having the required skills and experience. Those fears are probably justified: we were told about client organisations saving money by buying in one training course but from then on using the same programme and materials to train other staff themselves.

Most of the trainers we spoke to felt that courses are more effective if an ethnic minority trainer is involved. Some said this was because minority trainers helped to dispel stereotypes about black leadership and stopped white trainees from appealing to the assumed prejudices of the trainer. Others said that it was not simply the presence of the minority trainer that is useful, but rather the substantive input that a black trainer can make: a minority perspective is important to a successful course. However, many spoke of the pitfalls of setting minority trainers the impossible task of representing black people to the course: if trainees treat them as ethnic experts then an 'us and them' approach will prevail and the course will fail.

Bad behaviour

All the trainers said they sometimes encounter difficulties with course participants. The sensitivity of the subject matter means that individuals and groups can feel threatened and respond disruptively, by verbally attacking the trainers, by becoming abusive or sarcastic, or by refusing to participate, becoming quieter and less co-operative as the course develops. A majority of trainers said that they usually let the other participants deal with individual disrupters, because most people want to be on the courses and are interested in the issues. Where people cannot not be talked into co-operation, trainers take differing approaches: some just ignore the 'quiet resigners' but insist that trainees who are positively disruptive should leave the course, while other trainers continue with only those willing to participate actively. A majority, however, said that the willing trainees are their priority, and that it is a waste of effort to spend time trying to win over people with firmly racist views who want to disrupt the course.

Adverse reactions are more problematical when they come from several trainees or a whole group. Often a trainer is dealing with people who know each other and work together, and at difficult points they can rebel together. To keep things going trainers say they need to be firm but not inhumane; the firmness is required because the 'rebellion' often takes the form of challenging the credentials of the trainers, particularly black and women trainers, and can be personally probing and quite unpleasant. One trainer said that at the beginning of each course she gives the participants a prediction that they will try to undermine the trainers at some point. A common problem is that trainees try to play one trainer off against another, especially if they are a multi-racial team; trainers said it was vital to be on guard for this and avoid showing any friction – even if they do have a disagreement. In general, however, trainers do not complain that disruptions and challenges add up to more than minor irritations, and despite being personally fatiguing they do not present substantive obstacles to achieving training objectives.

5　Measuring Outcomes

The problem of evaluation

From our surveys of trainers and clients there was little evidence of serious attempts at evaluation of the contribution of race relations training to the achievement of specific or general equality objectives. Our informants pointed out that it is very difficult to envisage a way of telling how much the training, as opposed to other measures, affects the way employees and organisations change. However, even if one accepts that evaluation will always fall a long way short of this, it is still perhaps the area of greatest confusion and least systematic action. Indeed, one reason for its relative neglect could be an unwillingness to acknowledge that it cannot give an absolute answer, and a consequent paralysis over developing evaluation systems from which one could expect useful but less grand results. Many of our informants, trainers and clients alike, suggested that the training in which they were involved had not been 'properly' evaluated, as if it were an area in which their courses were deficient when compared with others. Their view was that direct evaluation is feasible but they have been unable to do it; we argue in this chapter that, on the contrary, direct evaluation is not feasible, but the evaluation tools already in use are of value.

Many informants talked about appraisal of the whole equal opportunities effort, usually in terms of ethnic monitoring, targets, and profiles of employees and customers. When we asked whether any evaluation of the training itself had taken place, the most frequently mentioned evaluation tool was the self-completion form handed out at the end of the course. This kind of form usually asks participants to score various aspects of the course on a rating scale and to express their general views about its merits and any problems. Most of our informants were sceptical about its value in telling whether a course has achieved its aims, but said they do find it useful for amending and improving the running of courses, and identifying elements that cause problems for trainees. One reason why the information is of limited value is that individual trainees may like course for reasons that have nothing to do with its impact in terms of their own learning or changes in the way they work; similarly a negative response may be elicited by an uncomfortable course which challenges a participant's work practice in exactly the way intended.

On many courses the trainees develop a personal or sectional action plan. Where the resources are available, this can be used as an aid to follow-up and evaluation: six months later the trainees can be asked about their progress on the action plan. Other in-service monitoring is also used to see what effects courses have: line managers are asked formally or informally about changes in the subsequent work of trainees.

> There were several methods of evaluation. There were questionnaires filled out by those who received training - more than your usual 'happy sheet.' Part of the training involved drawing up an action plan and setting a timetable. Line managers were responsible for seeing action plans were implemented.
> (Charitable organisation)

> The monitoring is now beginning to show the results of the equal opportunity policies. Last year we achieved seven and a half per cent ethnic minority recruitment. Ten per cent of graduate recruitment is ethnic minorities, and 50 per cent women. Now we want to target areas where it should be higher.
> (Large Finance Company)

During the course of the surveys we began to ask questions about the evaluation of other types of training in organisations. It appears that the agonizing over how to evaluate equal opportunities training is not matched by an interest in evaluating other types of training: very little evaluation of any training takes place. Perhaps this is because there is a general acceptance by employers that training is a necessary and acceptable part of staff development; the value of training per se is not therefore called into question. Equal opportunities training appears to be treated in a different way: as noted in Chapter 2, it is called to account in a way that other training is not.

Given these problems, it is worth unpicking the tangle of threads that make up the notion of evaluation. There seems to be a number of different things that we might want to measure, depending to some extent on the aims of the training. The list that follows may not be exhaustive, but it does show that the effects of training cannot be conceived of as one-dimensional; and all of the items on the list have been assessed by one or more organisations in our survey.

Evaluation: Possible Indicators

a. trainees' knowledge of the legislation and related concepts

b. trainees' knowledge about their specific work duties in terms of equal opportunities

c. trainees' beliefs about minority groups, women, race relations and other equal opportunities matters

d. trainees' skills pertaining to equal opportunities (e.g interviewing)

e. how well courses work, in terms of trainees' reactions, likes and dislikes

f. the extent to which trainees feel antipathy towards racial minority groups and other disadvantaged groups

g. on-the-job equality performance of individual trainees

h. equality performance of a department or a whole organisation

i. the policy and structure of a department or a whole organisation

Items (a) to (e) can be measured with some expectation of useful information pertaining to a particular training course or programme, using 'before and after' questionnaires (or, in the case of (e), simply a post-course questionnaire); they cannot, however, give direct evidence of improved equality performance. Changes in (g) to (i) can be measured as part of an organisation's comprehensive monitoring programme, but they do not necessarily help evaluate the contribution of training to the success of the overall equal opportunity package – though over time they might deliver some significant clues to this. As regards (f), the measurement of underlying racial antipathy, there is little hope of any valid 'before and after' test since a course would teach trainees the acceptable ways of saying things, irrespective of the tenacity of their personal feelings.

In summary, it would seem that it is practicable to evaluate the extent to which particular training courses achieve some of their short-term aims, but not their long-term equality outcomes; and it is practicable to evaluate outcomes of overall equal opportunity programmes, but not the special contribution that the training makes to these. All of these assessments have value, but it is important to recognise what they are and what they are not. Except in informal, impressionistic terms, it is not possible to assess directly whether a training course 'works' in terms of improvements in equality performance of a department or organisation.

The contribution of individual trainers

With any course that relies on people to engage with participants on difficult issues, success is dependent on the skills, experience and abilities of the trainers; and in every field of education and training, a poor teacher can make a mess of a good syllabus, while a good teacher can take a dull or inappropriate syllabus and build a valuable learning experience on it. Equal opportunities training is no exception, and our interviews suggest that some of the generalisations about its value and its problems have been based on limited experiences with trainers, among whom there is a range of skills and abilities as there is among any group of professionals. Again we should make the point that people do not usually judge whole fields of training activity on the basis of a single experience: people would not assess the value of health and safety training, or keyboard skills training, on the basis of observing one course. Equality trainers feel that they are too readily judged as a whole group.

External and internal trainers

The jolt that training can give to an organisation is more effective, according to some informants, if the trainers are outsiders. Compared with internal trainers, staff see them as more neutral, impartial, professional and removed from the politics of the organisation, and so they are able to operate with an immediately greater degree of credibility. The use of outside trainers is not without its problems, however. Because outsiders know less about the organisation than the staff, they can make mistakes or pitch the training at the wrong level; these dangers are of course reduced in proportion with the amount of collaborative planning and familiarisation that can be arranged between the client and provider.

Clients' appraisal of the training

The problems of evaluation described above mean that it is difficult to give any hard and fast answers about the contribution of race relations or equal opportunities training to the equality efforts of the organisations we visited. We have to rely on the views of the informants and our general impressions of the degree to which the training has been successful in these terms. To add to this difficulty, some of the organisations are at relatively early stages in their equal opportunities programme and their training programme, and therefore any assessments of outcomes are provisional.

Nevertheless, it is our strong impression that race relations and equal opportunities training has, in the majority of organisations we visited, had a beneficial outcome in terms of the development and implementation of equal opportunity programmes. The mechanisms by which the training has made its contribution vary from organisation to organisation, but that is to be expected, given the long list of activities that fall under the heading of race relations and equal opportunities training. For example, some have benefited by policy development, others by improvements in recruitment and selection procedures, and others by increased sensitivity of staff to the needs of minority ethnic clients. There were few examples of training going badly wrong, and in those cases other training measures were taken to put matters right.

Indicators of overall equality performance of organisations were mentioned by informants as showing, at least in part, the effect of training. Some organisations quoted the changes in the ethnic profile of their workforce and applicants for jobs. Some pointed out changes in the management of their organisation – such as the voluntary organisation that now has an improved representation of black people on its executive committee. Others said that there have been tangible improvements in the quality of service delivery: in the public sector, rules and procedures for dealing with clients have been revised, with the aim of reducing room for discrimination, and more attention has been paid to the careful translation of leaflets and publicity into minority languages; voluntary organisations said they now had better links with ethnic community groups, and had broadened their work to include previously ignored ethnic groups (for example, one scheme which deployed young people to carry out repairs to churches expanded their work to include mosques); and organisations in all sectors, including private companies, said they had changed their publicity and advertising material to reflect the multi-racial community. There is no doubt that a number of the employers we visited have seen considerable changes. Although, as suggested above, it is usually difficult to separate the contributions of different elements of the policy and programme, some informants made it clear that the training was a key part of the process:

> Training has worked to the extent that it has created a climate where the majority of white workers support the idea of rights for all workers. It's got a lot to do with training.
> (Local Authority)

> The courses were positively received and generated enthusiasm... The presentation was sophisticated and action plans were produced at the end... Attitudes were challenged and several people said that although they thought they knew enough already, attendance at the course had raised their awareness considerably. As tangible evidence, there has been a marked improvement in the writing of job descriptions and person specifications.
> (Higher Education Institution)

> You can see that after one day of training it is dawning on them that what they are doing is discriminatory.
> (Local Authority)

> People talk about it now, and they didn't before. We are getting more applications from ethnic minorities and more get offered jobs.
> (Large Minerals Company)

Some informants made less specific comments about the improvements that race relations training has led to, saying that staff have an improved sensitivity and feel for issues of race and discrimination, and that there have been clear improvements in the way things were done, although the improvements have not been measured – or are unmeasurable. For example, one informant said that two years ago staff were bewildered about taking on the issue of equality, but now they think it is part of their job, and they are capable of doing it. Often at least part of the aim of race relations training is changing the culture of an organisation, something which, if successful, can be felt but not measured. One informant talked of the training programme bringing their staff to a threshold of awareness about equal opportunities and thus enabling action; others said that things were being brought up, day to day, that never were before, and that queries related to equal opportunities were being referred to personnel and training departments. The injection of equal opportunities change into the culture of an organisation can have other, more general effects, too: some informants said that race relations training has been important to developing the momentum for other changes within the organisation.

For voluntary and community organisations, and to some extent in local authority departments, one result of race-related training seems be a change in their dealings with white clients: they are more likely to make a stand against racial abuse, harassment and exclusion. In some cases where staff were previously confused on the occasions when clients invited them to collude with racist views and even racist actions, the training equipped them to deal firmly with the problem. In some organisations this has been an important stage in opening up services and facilities to minority clients.

Sometimes another result of race related training and associated programmes is a heightened sense of identity among ethnic minority employees. In these cases it appears that the initiation of a discussion of racism and discrimination within an organisation allows people to voice common problems that were previously understood as individual difficulties. This process in turn becomes a further spur to the organisation's equal opportunities effort.

Although many informants said that training has led to improvements, some measurable and some not, in the equality performance of their organisations, others also reported satisfaction with the training but said there has been little actual progress on equal opportunities. They said that this is because other measures has not been sufficient to follow up the training with changes in the way their organisation works. This frustration was most common among specially appointed equal opportunities staff. They reminded us that there is a limit to what training can do, even if it is successful in its own terms, and that it could not work as a substitute for real organisational change.

6   Aiming for Equality

Training and organisational change

It has been a repeated theme of this study that training in race relations and equal opportunities refers not to a single type of employee training but embraces a wide range of activities. This can be gleaned from the commentaries on the history of race relations training, from the demands and experiences of the client organisations we visited, and from the services offered by the trainers we interviewed. One of the most important distinctions to make between different meanings of 'race relations training' is between training seen as an input to overall organisational change and training seen as a sprucing-up of staff performance. Despite its place within an overall context of formal equal opportunities policies, much of the recruitment and selection training that we found in this study is of the latter type. There is little doubt that training to improve interviewing and selection procedures does have an immediate equal opportunities impact, but the impact is limited. Some organisations take on programmes of equal opportunities training that are much more comprehensive. They do this by using training to look at ways in which their general structures, policies and practices have implications for race equality and can be improved. In some cases, these training programmes are accompanied by professional equal opportunities consultancy.

Other differences between types of training have been discussed in this report. Staff training in large industrial and commercial firms tends to focus on employment, personnel and staff development, and on staff skills and duties, while in public service and retail organisations the scope of training also covers client service and is often extended to include knowledge about minority experiences and cultures. These are only generalisations about the training we know about, but they are useful indicators that the diversity of training packages reflects a real diversity of needs and training aims. This analysis stands in contrast to the view that the diversity of training results from a confused set of approaches to a single training aim.

Establishing training aims

Given the range of options open to an organisation in terms of equal opportunities training, and given that the range is based on differences of training aims, what can we say about the process by which organisations choose, and should choose, from the options? The process so far has not been uniform, but it would be wrong to say that it has been haphazard, for we can see regularities within different categories of organisation, sometimes resulting from the direction of pressure for change (such as the more fundamental organisational measures in public sector and charitable bodies, as a consequence of justice-oriented equal opportunities approaches) and sometimes in line with the nature of the client organisation or department (such as the differences between equality training in employment and service delivery, as outlined above). It has also differed according to the sector of the training provider, partly because of the ability of trainers with background funding to spend more time on advice, consultancy and general organisational development, and partly because of the different professional and political histories of the trainers involved. Despite these patterns, it is also true that some organisations have blundered into equal opportunities training without explicit aims, and without any considered strategy of equal opportunities change.

How should training needs and training aims be established? If we start from a desire to maximise the equality performance of an organisation, in whatever area it is practicable, be it recruitment, staff development or customer service, then the training requirements must rest on an assessment of two things: first, the present shortcomings of its equality performance, and second, the changes necessary to improve that performance. Some of those are likely to be changes in work practices within the organisation, but others may be structural changes in the organisation itself. Depending on these assessments, a 'training' programme could be established with the right balance of organisational development, consultancy, high-level workshops, and staff training of different types. But who is to make the assessments? It is doubtful that they can be made accurately and comprehensively from within an organisation, because people on the inside have a view which is permeated by the very problems that they are concerned to tackle, so an outside view is also required. Independent trainers offer advice and consultancy in this area but, given the variation between different trainers in the substantive areas of their expertise, there is a risk that a client would be pulled towards the type of training in which the consultant is most interested (it should be remembered that this is not a problem unique to equal opportunities – it occurs in other fields where consultancy is bound up with provision, such as computing). It may be that a third, independent view is important. In principle this could come from a variety of sources – for example, from institutions such as the CRE, or the professional and employers' associations, from networks of organisations already involved in equal opportunities development, or from some kind of professional association of trainers. In practice there is a problem of resources, for none of these bodies could provide free advice and help without extra background funding. As we have seen in the surveys, employers are unlikely to relish the idea of direct spending on another layer of consultancy service, and most employers reduce the amount of pre-course consultation to a minimum, being prepared to go ahead on the basis of an independent needs assessment comprising only two or three meetings at managerial level.

However these problems of needs and aims assessment are resolved, one important conclusion of the study is that the variety of content and style of training on the market is sufficient to put the ball in the consumers' court. Employers report that training does play an important part in promoting equality in employment and in service delivery, but it has to be used for carefully planned strategic objectives within an overall programme. In the main, organisations are satisfied with the quality of training that has taken place, but there have been problems when the training objectives have been unclear or simply wrong for the organisation, and when training is expected to carry the entire burden of change. The important question is therefore not whether equal opportunities training as such is any good, but this: what types of training are necessary and appropriate to help the organisation implement a programme of equal opportunities change?

Promoting investment in equal opportunities
Another practical issue is the relationship between what an organisation needs and what it is prepared to do. Starting an analysis with the objective of maximising equality performance is helpful in

principle, but not all organisations are prepared to devote resources to a comprehensive equality programme, or to withstand the disruption that it might involve. Although there is a good business case to be made for equal opportunities, employers judge that there is a level of activity beyond which equality performance has a net cost in the short and medium term. Some firms take the view that their social responsibilities extend beyond this, and push their level of effort further for justice-oriented reasons, but our research does not suggest that they are common. In the public, charitable and voluntary sectors, where fairness is meant to be a central operational principle, pressure based largely on justice-oriented arguments can be applied and there are often several channels for that pressure. Above all, in those sectors the people who have power are publicly accountable and their decision-making is open to scrutiny. When pressed to change policy and practice for the better, they find they have to argue the matter in public. In the private sector, however, we were told repeatedly by informants that a business reason is required for all decisions, and that a simple argument about justice has little effect.

The main business-oriented arguments for developing equal opportunities programmes and training should be enumerated here. On the employment side, the most prominent argument is the growing shortage of job applicants and the consequent need to widen the recruitment pool. This has generally replaced the earlier, weaker argument that discriminatory recruitment, biased promotion and restrictive staff development prevent a company from realising the full potential of its current employees or the available labour force. The point about staff potential may be valid, but its appeal is based on marginal gains that are not easy to visualise, and its power to persuade is limited; staff shortages, on the other hand, are brutally convincing. Many of the employers we interviewed said that they were prompted to think about their recruitment procedures by a shortage or by the fear of shortages to come. The 'demographic downturn' has begun to affect employers, and they are now competing for staff, but in time things will get worse for them.

> We are experiencing huge recruitment problems. It's easy to identify how horrendous it will be when the number of school leavers drops more. We are having dedicated equal opportunities courses for managers at the right time.
> (Utility Company)

Previously neglected and badly-treated potential recruits, such as women and ethnic minorities, are now courted. In a number of cases the equal opportunities efforts of large companies began with a focus on the recruitment and retention of women, the largest source of potential labour, and turned later to ethnic minorities. Very recently, however, the underlying demographic trend towards labour shortage has been mitigated by an economic downturn which has raised the level of unemployment. It is unclear whether this will have a dampening effect on employers' attempts to widen the scope of their recruitment or the process will continue despite short-term economic fluctuations.

Another business-oriented motivation for equality measures starts with minorities, however, and that is the realisation of ethnic minority markets. The buying power and commercial clout of black and Asian people is being recognised, and some retail and financial companies are already competing for that business. Several told us that they were seeking to change their public image to appeal to ethnic minority customers, and that the change of image had to be carried through the whole organisation.

> Most people are coming in from the justice angle, and you can't sell
> it solely on that. Some firms are worried about shortages and are
> discovering ethnic markets, however.
> (Independent Trainer)

Another business argument for equal opportunities training is the avoidance of trouble with the Race Relations Act. Several employers told us that industrial tribunal cases are expensive and by comparison training is cheap. The loss of public face in such cases is also seen as a problem, particularly to those wanting to expand business with black customers, or with trading links overseas.

Training providers, when seeking to persuade employers to adopt equal opportunities measures, also appeal to the professionalism of managers, especially those working in personnel. They also argue that poor race relations in an organisation can inhibit other necessary changes. In a similar vein, some of the employer interviews suggested that openings for equal opportunities changes are created by the pace of other changes in industrial relations, technology or organisational structure.

The larger companies that have set out to improve their equality performance do say that public image is one of the factors that prompted them, and that a momentum develops in a particular industry. There is more to it than a bandwagon effect: sometimes a particular corporate policy stance becomes the norm by a curious interplay between politics and commercial competition, such as in the case of the current prominence of 'green' issues in company image-making. That process may have made a faltering start for equal opportunities in some areas, and has been encouraged by the establishing of informal networks of equal opportunities staff in private sector as well as in the public sector. Responsibility for the growth of that momentum rests both in the organisations that have made some progress already, and among people and bodies with the political power to convince employers equally of the business advantages of equal opportunities change and of the need for fairness and justice.

Bibliography

Ahmed, Shama, 'Some approaches to recruitment and in-service training for multiracial social work', *Social Work and Ethnicity*, Juliet Cheetham (ed.), George Allen and Unwin, 1982.

Ahmed, Shama, 'Let's break through the barriers to equality', *Community Care*, 1987, 29 October.

Ahmed, Shama, Hallett, Christine, Statham, Daphne and Watt, Shantu, 'A code of practice', *Community Care*, 1987, 29 October.

Alibhai, Yasmin, 'The reality of race training', *New Society*, 1988, 29 January.

All London Teachers Against Racism and Fascism, *Challenging Racism*, ALTARF, 1984.

Association of Scientific Technical and Managerial Staffs, *Race and Racism: a guide for ASTMS members*, 1984.

Bainbridge, Christine, 'Pilot study of racism awareness training', *The Police Journal*, 1984, April-June, vol. LVII, no. 2.

Baker, Phil and Hoadley-Maidment, Elizabeth, 'The social psychology of prejudice: an introduction', summary of the paper given at the 1979 Annual Conference, National Centre for Industrial Language Training, 1980.

Banton, Michael, *Police and Community Relations*, Collins, 1973.

Banton, Michael, 'Race, prejudice and education: changing approaches', *New Community*, vol. X, 3, Commission for Racial Equality, 1983.

Banton, Michael, 'RAT: back to the drawing board', *New Community*, vol. 7, no. 2, Commission for Racial Equality, 1985.

Beck, Jimmy, 'How the Met sees racism', *Police Review*, 1987, 10 July.

Bull, Ray and Horncastle, Peter, *An Evaluation of the Metropolitan Police Recruit Training in Human Awareness*, The Police Foundation, 1983.

Cabinet Office (Management and Personnel Office), *Be Fair: an equal opportunities resource manual*, Institute of Personnel Management/British Association for Commercial and Industrial Education, 1987.

Campaign Against Racism and Fascism, 'The politics of racism awareness training', *Searchlight*, 1985, February.

Campaign Against Racism and Fascism, 'The RAT race: degrading black struggle', *Searchlight*, 1985, March.

Cannan, Crescy, 'Social work, race relations and the social work curriculum', *New Community*, vol. 7, nos. 1/2, Commission for Racial Equality, 1983.

Carby, Keith and Thakur, Manab, *No Problems Here?*, Institute of Personnel Management, 1977.

Carter, Anne (ed.), *Teachers for a Multicultural Society*, Schools Curriculum Development Council Publications, 1985.

Central Council for Education and Training in Social Work, *Teaching Social Work for a Multi-racial Society: Report of a working group*, CCETSW paper 21: Social work curriculum study, 1983.

Central Council of Probation Committees, *Probation: a multi-racial approach*, 1983.

Chesler, Mark and Delgado, Hector, 'Race relations training and organisational change', *Strategies for Improving Race Relations: The Anglo-American experience*, Shaw, John, Nordlie, Peter and Shapiro, Richard (eds.), Manchester University Press, 1987.

Christmas, Elisa, *A Study and Experiment in Race Awareness Training for Metropolitan Police Probationers*, National Centre for Industrial Language Training, 1983.

Coffey, John, 'Race training in the United States: an overview', *Strategies for improving race relations: the Anglo-American experience*, Shaw, John, Nordlie, Peter and Shapiro, Richard (eds.), Manchester University Press, 1987.

Community Care, 'A basically racist society', 1983, March 31.

Community Relations Commission, *Teacher Education for a Multi-Cultural Society*, 1974.

Community Relations Commission, *In-service Education for Teachers in Multi-Racial Areas: An evaluation of current practice*, 1974.

Community Relations Commission, *Training nursery teachers in a multi-cultural society: National Seminar 7-8 February 1975*, 1975.

Community Relations Commission, *Social work training in a multi-racial society: Report of a conference held on 21-23 September 1976*, 1976.

Community Relations Commission, *Training Nursery Nurses for a Multi-Racial Community: Report on seminar for NNEB tutors 6-8 February 1976*, 1976.

Conway, Edmund, 'Trade union studies for immigrants', *Adult Education*, 49(4), 1986, November.

Coombe, Vivienne and Little, Alan, *Race and Social Work: A guide to training*, Cambridge University Press, 1986.

Coopers and Lybrand Associates, *Industrial Language Training Study: Final report*, 1985, December.

Commission for Racial Equality, *Local Authorities and the Education Implications of Section 71 of the Race Relations Act 1976*, 1981, August.

Commission for Racial Equality, *Report of Joint Commission for Racial Equality/Police Community Relations Training Working Party*, 1981, December.

Commission for Racial Equality, *Local Government Training and Racial Equality: A report of a series of seven regional seminars held in May-June 1983*, 1983, November.

Commission for Racial Equality, *A Report on the Seminar on Racism Awareness Training, October 1984*, 1985.

Commission for Racial Equality, *Swann: A response from the Commission for Racial Equality*, 1985, October.

Commission for Racial Equality, *Training: The implementation of equal opportunities at work: Volume 1: Policy and Planning*, 1987.

Commission for Racial Equality, *Training: The implementation of equal opportunities at work: Volume 2: Case Studies*, 1987.

Commission for Racial Equality, *Training for Equality at Work: A report of seminars held in London and Birmingham, May 1988*, 1988.

Commission for Racial Equality, *Training for Racial Equality in Housing: A guide*, 1989.

Commission for Racial Equality, *Action Planning and Training for Racial Equality: Report of a conference for training managers on 7 June 1989 at the University of Warwick*, 1989.

Commission for Racial Equality and West Midlands County Probation and After-Care Service, *Probation and After-care in a Multi-Racial Society*, 1981, May.

Commission for Racial Equality, *Training: Implementing Racial Equality at Work: A Curriculum Guide*, 1991.

Cridland, Wyn, 'Human awareness training for the police', *The Police Journal*, 1984, January-March, vol. LVII, no. 1.

Crofts, Paul, *Report on the Police Training Experiment*, Ealing Community Relations Council, 1982.

Das, P.K., 'State-mandated training in police community relations: an evaluation', *Police Journal*, vol. LX, no. 3, 1987, July.

Davies, A., 'Racism awareness training: What's it all about?', *Voluntary Action*, 1984, June.

Department of Education and Science, *The Education of Immigrants*, Education Survey 13, HMSO, 1971.

Department of Health and Social Security, *The Employment and Training of Linkworkers: training manual*, 1988.

Dolan, John, '"Multicultural education" for whom?', *New Community*, vol. X, no. 3, Commission for Racial Equality, 1983.

Dummett, Ann, 'Practical anti-racism', *New Society*, 1987, April 10.

Easterby-Smith, Mark and Tanton, Mary, 'Turning course evaluation from an end to a means', *Personnel Management*, 1985, April.

Edmunds, Juliet and Powell, Diana, 'Are you a racist too?', *Community Care*, 1985, September 19.

Ely, Peter and Denney, David, *Social Work in a Multi-Racial Society*, Gower, 1987.

Ferne, Peter, 'Mobilising the grassroots of anti-racism', *Social Work Today*, 1990, 8 March.

Fidler, John, 'Constant vigilance breeds colour harmony', *The Engineer*, 1973, 14 June.

Fielding, N.G., *The Development of the Attitudes of Police Recruits During Training: ESRC end of grant report*, Economic and Social Research Council, 1984.

Firth, Ralph and Channer, Yvonne, 'Progress on the path to anti-racism', *Social Work Today*, 1989, November 16.

Gaine, Chris, *No Problem Here: A practical approach to education and 'race' in white schools*, Hutchinson, 1987.

Gilbert, John, 'Fighting racism - an optimist and a realist', *Social Work Today*, 1988, 7 January.

Greater London Council, *Policing London: The policing aspects of Lord Scarman's Report on the Brixton Disorders*, 1982.

Greater London Council, *Training for Change: the GLC's equal opportunities and positive action programme*, 1988.

Goldin, Paul C., 'A model for racial awareness training of teachers in integrated schools', *Integrated Education*, 1970, January-February.

Gordon, Paul, *Anti-racist Materials for Adult and Community Education*, Runnymede Trust, 1986.

Gordon, Paul and King, Francesca, *Racism and Discrimination in Britain: A select bibliography 1970-83*, Runnymede Trust, 1984.

Greater London Action on Race Equality, *No Alibi, No Excuse*, 1987.

Gurnah, Ahmed, 'The politics of racism and awareness training', *Critical Social Policy*, issue 11, 1984.

Hackett, Geraldine and Paddison, Loraine, 'Who'd be an equal opportunity manager', *Personnel Management*, 1988, April.

Hall, Trevor, 'Race relations training: a personal view', *New Directions in Police Training*, Southgate, Peter (ed.), HMSO, 1988.

Harris, Vernon, 'Changing minds: reply to article by Margaret Jervis', *Social Services Insight*, 1987, July 17.

Health Education Council/National Extension College for Training in Health and Race, *Providing Effective Health Care in Multi-Racial Society: A checklist for looking at local issues*, Health Education Council, 1984.

Hincliffe, Margaret, 'Teaching English to Asian men and women', *New Community*, vol. 4, no. 3, Commission for Racial Equality, 1975.

Holden, Tony, *People, Churches and Multi-Racial Projects: An account of English Methodism's response to plural Britain*, The Methodist Church, Division of Social Responsibility, 1985.

House of Commons, Home Affairs Committee, *Racial Disadvantage*, Fifth Report of the Home Affairs Committee, HMSO, 1981.

Housing Training Project, *Housing Work in Multi-Racial Areas: A review of training approaches and resources*, City University, 1980.

Inner London Education Authority, *Race, Sex and Class: 2. Multi-Ethnic Education in Schools*, 1983.

Iles, Paul and Auluck, Randhir, 'From racism awareness training to strategic human resource management in implementing equal opportunity', *Personnel Review*, 18,4, 1989.

Jervis, Margaret, 'RATs tales', *Social Services Insight*, 1986, July 12 -July 19.

Jervis, Margaret, 'The thorny question of anti-racism', *Social Work Today*, 1987, 9 November.

Judge, A., 'The police and coloured communities', *New Community*, vol. III, no. 3, Commission for Racial Equality, 1974.

Judges, Bob, 'Racism: the Birmingham strategy', *Social Work Today*, 1987, May 11.

Katz, Judy, *White Awareness: Handbook for anti-racism training*, University of Oklahoma Press, 1978.

Katz, Judy and Ivey, Allen, 'White awareness: the frontier of racism awareness training', *Personnel and Guidance Journal*, 1977, April.

Kelvyn Richards, J., 'A contribution to the multicultural education debate', *New Community*, vol. X, no. 2, Commission for Racial Equality, 1982.

Kinnon, Usha, 'Racism awareness - Who helps the client?', *Journal of Social Work Practice*, vol. 3, no. 3, 1988.

La Fontaine, Jean, 'Countering racial prejudice: a better starting-point', *New Community*, vol. 8, no. 3, Commission for Racial Equality, 1987.

Labour Research Department, *Black Workers, Trade Unions and the Law: A negotiator's guide*, LRD publications, 1985.

Ladbury, Sarah, 'Equal opportunities training', *New Society*, 1987, 6 November.

Lee, Gloria, 'Implementing equal opportunity: a training perspective', *Equal Opportunities International*, 2,1, pp.27-36, 1983.

Lee, Gloria, 'Training and organisational change: the target racism', *Racism and Equal Opportunity Policies in the 1980s*, Jenkins, Richard and Solomos, John (eds.), Cambridge University Press, 1987.

Lee, Gloria, 'Does training matter?', Anti-discrimination and equal opportunity in employment workshop, University of Aston, 1983, June.

Lena, Dominelli, *Anti-racist social work*, Macmillan, 1988.

Lightfoot, Martin, 'Community and race relations training', *New Directions in Police Training*, Southgate, Peter (ed.), HMSO, 1988.

Little, Alan and Willey, Richard, *Multi-Ethnic Education: The way forward*, Schools Council Pamphlet 18, Schools Council, 1981.

Local Government Training Board, *Training Implications of the CRE Code of Practice*, 1982.

Local Government Training Board, *Directory of Race Relations and Equal Opportunities Trainers*, 1987.

London Strategic Policy Unit, *Racism Awareness Training - A Critique*, 1987.

Lunn, Tim, 'Sensitive to people's needs', *Community Care*, 1987, 5 November.

Mahon, Tom, 'When line managers welcome equal opportunities', *Personnel Management*, 1989, October.

Matthews, Arnold, *Advisory Approaches to Multicultural Education*, Runnymede Trust, 1981.

McIlroy, John, 'Educating the natives - race and workers education', *Adult Education*, 53(1), 1980, May.

McIlroy, John, 'Effective race relations training: some experience from industry', *New Community*, vol. 9, no. 1, Commission for Racial Equality, 1981.

McKenzie, Ian K., 'The essential requirements of his calling - police training in the 1980s', *The Police Journal*, 1984, vol. LVII, no. 3.

McKenzie, Ian K., 'Racism and the police service - where to now?', *The Police Journal*, 1986, vol. LVIX, no. 1.

Meager, Nigel and Metcalf, Hilary, *Equal Opportunities Polices: Tactical issues in implementation*, Institute of Manpower Studies, 1988.

Miller, H., 'The effectiveness of teaching techniques for reducing colour prejudice', *Liberal Education* 16, 1969, July.

Millins, P.K.C., 'The Rampton report and teacher education', *Secondary Education Journal*, vol. 11, no. 3, National Union of Teachers, 1981.

Munns, Roger and Strutt, Peter, 'Adult education in the workplace: values and conflicts in industrial language training', *Adult Education*, 53(2), 1980, July.

Murray, A.D. and Chandola, J.R., *Training for a Multiracial Society - A practitioner's approach*, National Centre for Industrial Language Training Working paper no. 26, 1981.

Murray, Alan and Chandola, J.R., 'Towards effective race relations training: response to Peppard's article', *New Community*, vol. 8, no. 3, Commission for Racial Equality, 1980.

National Association for the Care and Resettlement of Offenders Race Issues Advisory Committee, *Black People and the Criminal Justice System: Report of the NACRO race issues advisory committee*, NACRO, 1986.

National Black Group of Industrial Language Training Service, *Industrial Language Training in the 1990s: The black perspective*, 1986.

Newby, Tony, 'Training and race relations: 1. Formal interventions', *The Training Officer*, 1982, July.

Newby, Tony, 'Training and race relations: 2. Knowledge and skill-based approaches', *The Training Officer*, 1982, August.

Newby, Tony, 'Training and race relations: 3. Attitude change', *The Training Officer*, 1982, September.

NHS Training Authority, *Equal Opportunities: A training and resource pack*, 1989.

Nicod, Michael and Jackson, Anna, *Review of Industrial Language Training Service: Final report*, Manpower Services Commission, 1985.

Nordlie, Peter, 'The evolution of race relations training in the US army', *Strategies for Improving Race Relations: The Anglo-American experience*, Shaw, John, Nordlie, Peter and Shapiro, Richard (eds.), Manchester University Press, 1987.

Oakley, Robin, 'Community and race relations training for the police: a review of developments', *New Community*, vol. 16, no. 1, Commission for Racial Equality, 1989.

O'Brien, John and Gubbay, Denise, 'Training to integrate the multi-racial workforce', *Personnel Management*, 1979, January.

Oldfield, Carolyn, *Resources On and Against Racism: Information pack*, National Youth Bureau, 1989.

Ouseley, Herman, with Silverstone, Danny and Prashar, Usha, *The System*, Runnymede Trust and South London Equal Rights Consultancy, 1981.

Owsu-Bempah, J., 'Does colour matter?', 1989, 26 January.

Pearson, Maggie, 'Against the Grain', *Senior Nurse*, vol. 5, no. 5/6, 1986, November/December.

Peppard, Nadine, 'Towards effective race relations training', *New Community*, vol. 8, nos. 1/2, Commission for Racial Equality, 1980.

Peppard, Nadine, 'Race relations training: the state of the art', *New Community*, vol. 6, nos. 1/2, Commission for Racial Equality, 1983.

Peppard, Nadine, 'Race relations training: the Patrick experiment', *New Community*, vol. XI, no. 3, Commission for Racial Equality, 1984.

Phillips, Melanie and Fearns, Peter, 'Myth and reality in practice teaching', *Community Care*, 1987, October 29.

Police Training Council Working Party, *Community and Race Relations Training for the Police: Report of the Police Training Council Working Party*, Home Office, 1983.

Prashar, Usha, 'Evening up the odds for black workers', *Personnel Management*, 1983, June.

Pumfrey, Peter, D., 'Some reflections on racism awareness training', *New Community*, vol. 7, no. 3, Commission for Racial Equality, 1985-6.

Rampton, Anthony, *West Indian Children in our Schools: Interim report of the Committee of Inquiry into the education of children from ethnic minority groups*, HMSO, 1981.

Read, Jim, *The Equal Opportunity Book: A guide to employment practice in voluntary organisations and community groups*, InterChange Books, 1989.

Roberts, Celia, 'Industrial English language training for overseas workers', *New Community*, vol. 4, no. 3, Commission for Racial Equality, 1975.

Rose, E.J.B., *Colour and Citizenship: A report on British race relations*, Oxford University Press, 1969.

Rubber and Plastics Processing Industry Training Board, *Managing in the Multi-Racial Company*, 1979.

Runnymede Trust, *Ethnic Minorities in Britain: A select bibliography*, 1979.

Segar, Richard and Bunker, Ken, 'The training anlge', *Voluntary Housing*, 1989, January.

Shaw, John, 'Towards effective race relations training: response to Peppard's article', *New Community*, vol. 8, no. 3, Commission for Racial Equality, 1980.

Shaw, John, 'Training methods in race relations within organisations: an analysis and assessment', *New Community*, vol. IX, no. 3, Commission for Racial Equality, 1982.

Shaw, John, 'Planning and implementing race relations seminars: the Holly Royde experience', *Strategies for Improving Race Relations: The Anglo-American experience*, Shaw, John, Nordlie, Peter and Shapiro, Richard (eds.), Manchester University Press, 1987.

Shaw, John, 'The Holly Royde senior police seminar in community relations: 1986 to 1987'. *New Directions in Police Training*, Southgate, Peter (ed.), HMSO, 1988.

Shaw, John, Nordlie, Peter and Shapiro, Richard (eds.), *Strategies for Improving Race Relations: The Anglo-American experience*, Manchester University Press, 1987.

Shepherd, Eric, 'Values into practice: the implementation and implications of human awareness training', *The Police Journal*, 1984, vol. LVII, no. 3.

Shillan, David, 'A diploma in "Education for a Multicultural Society"', *New Community*, vol. 4, no. 3, Commission for Racial Equality, 1975.

Sivanandan, A., 'In the castle of their skin', *New Statesman*, 1985, 7 June.

Sivanandan, A., 'RAT and the Degradation of Black Struggle', *Race and Class*, vol. 25, no. 4, Institute of Race Relations, 1985.

Smith, Peter, 'Group process methods of intervention in race relations', *Strategies for Improving Race Relations: The Anglo-American experience*, Shaw, John, Nordlie, Peter and Shapiro, Richard (eds.), Manchester University Press, 1987.

Smith, Peter and Wilson, Michael, 'The use of group training methods in multi-racial settings', *New Community*, vol. IV, 2, Commission for Racial Equality, 1975.

Social Work Today, 'RAT package scrapped', 1987, March 16.

Southgate, Peter, *Police Probationer Training in Race Relations*, Home Office, Research and Planning Unit paper 8, 1982.

Southgate, Peter, *Racism Awareness Training for the Police*, Home Office, Research and Planning Unit paper 29, 1984.

Southgate, Peter (ed.), *New Directions in Police Training*, HMSO, 1988.

St. Claire-Ellice-Williams, Robert, 'On tape and in print', *Community Care*, 1987, 29 October.

Stiles, Jenny, 'Opening employment and training opportunities in community work', *Community Work and Racism*, Ohri, Manning and Curno (eds.), Routledge and Kegan Paul.

Straw, Jane, *Equal Opportunities: the way ahead*, Institute of Personnel Management, 1989.

Stubbs, Paul, 'The employment of black social workers: from "ethnic sensitivity" to anti-racism?', *Critical Social Policy*, 1985, issue 12.

Swann, Lord, *Education For All: A brief guide to the main issues of the report*, HMSO, 1985.

Swann, Lord, *Education For All: The report of the Committee of Inquiry into the education of children from ethnic minority groups*, HMSO, 1985.

Taylor Fitz-Gibbon, Carol, 'Peer tutoring: a possible method for multi-ethnic education', *New Community*, vol. 11, nos. 1/2, Commission for Racial Equality, 1983.

Taylor, Wendy, 'Race relations interventions within a probation service', *Strategies for improving race relations: the Anglo-American experience*, Shaw, John, Nordlie, Peter and Shapiro, Richard, Manchester University Press, 1987.

Thomson, Brenda, 'I am racism: multicultural education and racism awareness', *Secondary Education Journal*, vol. 11, no. 3, National Union of Teachers, 1981.

Tonkin, Boyd, 'State of the art', *Community Care*, 1987, 12 March.

Tonkin, Boyd, 'Where the town hall sets the pace', *Community Care*, 1987, 29 October.

Trades Union Congress, *TUC workbook on racism*, 1983.

Verma, Gajendra K. and Bagley, Christopher, 'Measured changes in racial attitudes following the use of three different teaching methods', *Race, Education and Identity*, Verma, Gajendra K. and Bagley, Christopher (eds.), Macmillan, 1979.

Wainwright, D., *Learning from Uncle Sam: Equal employment opportunity programme*, Runnymede Trust, 1980.

Wild, Alan, 'Realistic expectations of equal opportunities', *Personnel Management*, 1986, October.

Wilkinson, J.P., 'Why magistrates need race relations training', *New Community*, vol. 7, no. 3, Commission for Racial Equality, 1985-6.

Wilson, Amrit, 'Therapy for racism', *New Statesman*, 1984, July 13.

Yates, Valerie, *A proposal for a training development project for the Metropolitan Police*, National Centre for Industrial Language Training, 1982, April.

Yates, Valerie and Wilson, Peter, 'A real eye-opener: An account of a course in communications for supervisors', *The Training Officer*, 1987, November.

Yates, Valerie, Christmas, Elisa and Wilson, Peter, *Cross-cultural Training: Developing skills and awareness in communication: a manual for trainers*, National Centre for Industrial Language Training, 1982.

Yeboah, Freda and Palmer, Sarah, *The LARRIE catalogue*, Local Authorities Race Relations Exchange, 1987.

Young, John N., 'ILEA's anti-racism policy: a note', *New Community*, vol. xii, no. 1, Commission for Racial Equality, 1984-5.

Appendix I: The Telephone Survey of Employers

The telephone survey of employers was based on a random sample of private sector firms with over 100 employees, in the areas covered by the race relations training study: Greater London, the East and West Midlands, and West Yorkshire. The interviews, which used the schedule shown in Appendix II, lasted between five and twenty minutes. The achieved sample was 125 employers and the response rate was 66 per cent. Table A1 gives further details of the response.

The aim of the random sampling was not to generate an accurately representative sample of firms, but to ensure that inclusion of a wide range of different employers. The sample size is too small to generate numerical estimates of the extent of training in the private sector as a whole; rather, the intention is to present a general picture of the way race relations and equal opportunities training is seen in private firms, given that most of the training work that came to light in the other parts of the study is in the public and voluntary sectors.

Profile of the companies in the sample

As shown in Table A2, the manufacturing and engineering industries account for 44 companies in the survey (35 per cent), and the finance industry accounts for 29 (23 per cent). Compared with the national profile of firms of all sizes, the sample has proportionally fewer firms in the wholesale and retail sectors; this is probably a consequence of the exclusion of small firms. Over 40 per cent of the informants were in companies with 500 or more employees.

There is a wide range of employers in terms of the ethnic composition of the workforce. One in ten of the informants said that their establishment has no ethnic minority employees; but more than one in five said that their workforce is made up of at least 20 per cent ethnic minority employees.

Equal opportunities policies
We asked whether the companies have a written equal opportunities policy of any sort, and forty per cent said they have (Table A3). At the time of the survey, most of these policies had existed for over a year, but few of them had existed for more than five years. Most of the written policies are less than a page in length, and some comprise only a single sentence or paragraph; although this is a very crude measure, it does give an indication of the problem of classifying the seriousness with which employers take their equal opportunities responsibilities – a 'policy' is often a simple statement of the firm's legal obligations and an exhortation to staff to abide by them.

Equal opportunities policies seem in most cases to be implemented at a managerial level rather than at board level or by junior administrative staff. In over half of the firms with a policy the person responsible for overseeing its implementation and development is a manager with other human resources responsibility – a personnel manager or training manager, or the general administrative manager. In two cases the job is done by a specifically designated equal opportunities manager. In only two cases was a director in charge.

We detected no systematic differences between regions or industrial sectors, but the presence of an equal opportunities policy does seem to be related to the size of the company: bigger companies are more likely to have them.

Reasons for having no equal opportunities policy
The majority of informants in firms without an equal opportunities policy said that they do not need one: most said that equal opportunities is just not an issue, or there is no discrimination in their company, or they are already dealing with it in practice (Table A4).

Has equal opportunities ever been raised as an issue?
Firms without an equal opportunities policy were asked whether the issues of equal opportunities, race or sex discrimination had ever been brought up for formal discussion by a staff representative, a manager or anyone else. Only eight said that such issues had been discussed (Table A5). In three of those firms the outcome of the discussions is that a policy is currently being developed.

The CRE code of practice

When asked, two thirds of the informants said they had heard of the Race Relations Code of Practice produced by the Commission for Racial Equality, and one third said that their firm had received a copy (Table A6). One fifth have looked at the Code themselves.

Ethnic record keeping

Nearly a third of informants said their companies keep ethnic records on staff or job applicants (Table A7). This proportion is surprisingly high; furthermore, it is puzzling to note that firms with equal opportunities policies were no more likely than others to say that they keep ethnic records. Perhaps there was confusion over the terms used here: in the survey we asked about 'records of the ethnic origin of employees or job applicants', without giving any additional definitions, and it is possible that a number of informants assumed that they should include any records of birthplace or nationality. Eleven per cent said (unprompted) that they keep records of nationality.

Industrial tribunals

Only two informants said that their firm had ever had to deal with an industrial tribunal case alleging race or sex discrimination (Table A8).

Recruitment methods

Recruitment methods for manual staff, counter sales staff, office staff and management staff are shown in Table A9. For all types of job, over two-thirds of firms use advertisements in the press. Other methods are used in proportions that vary by the type of job: for example, Jobcentres are used by more than two-thirds of firms for manual staff, but less frequently for white-collar staff; employment agencies, however, are used often for office staff, but infrequently for manual staff and counter sales staff. Word-of-mouth recruitment was mentioned unprompted by less than a fifth of informants, and is more important for counter sales and manual staff than for office and managerial staff.

In the lower part of the table the recruitment methods for manual, office and managerial staff are shown separately for the firms known to have equal opportunities policies and for other firms (numbers for counter sales staff are too small to split up in this way). The differences are not great, but the firms with EO policies on average use a slightly higher number of methods for each job type, and are slightly more inclined to use the press, Jobcentres, agencies and internal recruitment than the other firms.

Training
Present training arrangements
Four basic questions were asked about the training activities of the employer in the areas of personnel management and equal opportunities: whether employees have had training in (a) recruitment and selection procedures; (b) other personnel aspects of management and administrative jobs; (c) employment laws; and (d) equal opportunities or race relations. The great majority of firms have staff trained in one or more of these areas; in fact about nine out of ten firms have staff trained in one or other of the first three areas (Table A10).

A substantial minority – one third of firms – also said they have staff who have received training regarding equal opportunities or race relations. This does not, however, mean that all of them have run specific courses for their staff on these issues; in fact very little of the activity mentioned in response to this question could be treated as race or equal opportunities training except in the most general sense. About half of them said that one or more staff had been on a course elsewhere that covered race or sex discrimination, or the relevant legislation; nearly all of these were general management, personnel management or employment law courses, and informants were fairly vague about the degree of emphasis that the training placed on equality issues (and, in some cases, about the whole affair – for example, one said she thought it was 'likely' that personnel officers have attended seminars that covered the issues, and another said she was not sure but 'expected' that it would form part of the external management training courses that staff attended). None of them said they had been on an external course specifically dealing with race equality.

Most of the others who said they have race or equal opportunities training provide it in-house, using their own trainers, and, like the external courses described above, usually provide it as part of a more general course on management or recruitment and selection. Again, none of them said that they have run a course specifically dealing with race equality. Two of the firms said that their training in the area amounted only to circulating information to staff to keep them up to date with legislation and other developments.

Only two employers said that outside trainers have come into the firm to run a course on race relations or equal opportunities: one had taken on an independent consultant and the other had used RREAS. Both of these firms had training sessions for managers, and one of them extended the training to supervisors. Both said they were satisfied with the training, although one of them commented that a problem with all outside trainers was that they covered some areas that their staff already knew about. Both firms have had equal opportunities policies for more than a year, although neither keeps ethnic records of employees or applicants (one of the informants, a personnel director, thought that keeping such records was racial discrimination).

Seventeen firms said they have had some contact with RREAS, and four said have had some contact with an ILT unit (Table A11). Some of the informants were a little confused about the distinctions between the CRE, RREAS and the ILTUs, despite our explanation of the differences. Of the 17 RREAS contacts, 13 said they have an equal opportunities policy.

Training needs
About 40 per cent of the informants feel that there is a need for staff training in their firm in the area of selection, recruitment and personnel; the figure is the same for training in employment law (Table A12). One third of informants feel there is a need for training in equal opportunities and race relations. Of the 80 informants who said that their company has no training in equal opportunities or race relations, 19 feel that there is a need for it (24 per cent).

Reasons for not thinking something are always hard to elicit reliably in surveys, but we did ask informants why they felt their company needs no training in equal opportunities or race relations, and the majority said they thought their present arrangements are sufficient, or that they provide equal opportunities already. These responses accord closely with the reasons that informants gave for their firm having no equal opportunities policy.

Training and equal opportunities policies
Half of the firms with equal opportunities policies had some kind of race relations or equal opportunities training, compared with less than a quarter of the rest (Table A13). Among those with a policy but no

training, two fifths said the training was needed. All of the informants who felt that there was no need for training said it was because their firms had no equal opportunities problems or their present arrangements were satisfactory.

Table A1 Details of survey: sample numbers, response rate and person interviews

		numbers
a.	Sample drawn	211
b.	Firms later rejected (too small etc.)	23
c.	Actual sample (a-b)	188
d.	Non-contacts	17
e.	Refusals	37
f.	Other non-response	11
g.	Total contacts (c-d)	174
h.	Refusal rate (e/g)	21%
i.	TOTAL INTERVIEWS	125
j.	Overall response rate (i/c)	66%
Person Interviewed		
Company Director		7
Equal Opportunities Manager		1
Personnel/Training/Office Manager		55
Other Management		15
Other Personnel Staff		23
Secretarial/Support Staff		24

Table A2 Profile of employers: region, industry, size and ethnic composition of workforce

numbers

Region	
London	77
E Midlands	21
W Midlands	17
W Yorks	10
Industry	
Energy	3
Minerals	5
Engineering	13
Manufacturing	31
Construction	10
Wholesale, Retail	19
Transport, Communications	3
Finance	29
Other Services	12
Number of employees in UK	
100-199	36
200-499	36
500-999	18
1000-4999	24
5000+	7
Not known	4
Number of establishments in UK	
1 24	
2-435	
5-929	
10-49	22
50-97	5
98+	6
Not known	4
Employees of ethnic minority origin at establishment	
None	12
Under 5%	35
5-9%	16
10-19%	20
20-49%	19
50%+	9
Not known	14
TOTAL	125

Table A3 Does firm have a written equal opportunities policy of any sort?

numbers

Yes	49
No'	61
Don't know	15
TOTAL	125

IF YES:
Length of written policy?
- less than one page   35
- more than one page   3
- don't know   11

Had it for how long?
- less than a year   5
- more than a year   29
- more than five years   7
- don't know   8

Who has responsibility for overseeing development and implementation?
- personnel/training/admin manager   29
- personnel dept   5
- company director   2
- equal opps manager   2
- support staff   2
- consultative committee   1
- 'devolved responsibility'   1
- don't know   7

Who initiated original discussions?
- personnel manager/personnel section   7
- other manager   3
- company director   3
- unions   3
- ACAS   1
- other external pressure   3
- don't know   29

Company size and equal opportunities policies:

	Percentage with an EO policy
100-199 employees	24%
200-999 employees	43%
1000+ employees	55%

Table A4 Why is it that the firm has no policy or statement on equal opportunities?

numbers

Not an issue	23
No discrimination	15
Already deal with it in practice	12
Employ people from varied backgrounds	5
Company too small	4
Other reason	5
Couldn't say	11
TOTAL	75

Table A5 Has the issue of equal opportunities, race or sex discrimination ever formally discussed in firm?

numbers

Already have equal opps policy	49
No policy, but have discussed the issue	8
No policy, no discussion of issue	68

IF NO POLICY BUT HAVE DISCUSSED THE ISSUE
Who brought it up?

- personnel manager/section	2
- other manager	3
- don't know	3

Outcome

- policy being developed	3
- don't know	5

Table A6 Knowledge of the CRE Race Relations Code of Practice

	numbers
Had heard of the Code of Practice	82
... and knew firm had received the Code	43
... and had looked at the Code	24
... and had read through the Code	21
TOTAL	125

Table A7 Does firm keep records of ethnic origin of employees or job applicants?

	numbers
Keeps ethnic records	37
Keeps records of nationality only	14
No ethnic or nationality records	71
Don't know	3
TOTAL	125

Table A8 Has firm ever had to deal with industrial Tribunal case over race or sex discrimination?

	numbers
Yes	2
No	113
Don't know	10
TOTAL	125

Table A9   Recruitment methods

Column percentages

	Manual staff	Counter staff	Office staff	Managerial staff
Prompted responses				
Press adverts	72	72	80	71
Jobcentre	72	41	54	44
Agency	27	21	74	60
Unprompted responses				
Word of mouth	16	21	6	7
Unsolicited	11	3	2	4
Internal	3	14	7	20
Other	10	7	5	11
Base (= all recruiting these staff grades)	88	29	123	123

(EO = firm has equal opps policy No EO = other firms)	Manual staff		Office staff		Managerial stall	
	EO	No EO	EO	No EO	EO	No EO
Prompted responses						
Press	75	71	81	77	75	69
Jobcentre	75	69	63	48	15	11
Agency	33	23	75	72	65	57
Unprompted responses						
Word of mouth	14	17	4	6	4	6
Unsolicited	11	12	4	-	6	3
Internal	8		13	4	25	17
Other	6	13		8	13	11
Average number of methods mentioned	2.2	2.1	2.4	2.2	2.0	1.7
Base (all companies recruiting these staff grades)	36	52	48	75	48	75

Table A10 Are managers and employees trained in personnel matters and equal opportunities?

	numbers
Yes, recruitment and selection	83
Yes, other personnel aspects	75
Yes, employment laws	78
Yes, equal opps/race relations	40
Yes, any of the above	109
TOTAL	125

Table A11 Contact with RREAS and ILTS

	numbers
Had contact with RREAS only	15
Had contact with ILTS only	2
Had contact with both	2
No contact with either	99
Don't know	7
TOTAL	125

Table A12 Perceived need for staff training

numbers

Need selection, recruitment, personnel training	48
Need employment law training	49
Need equal opportunities and race relations training	34
TOTAL	125

Reasons for not needing eo/rr training-
(only those who have no such training in their firm)

not an issue	10
we provide equal opps	13
present arrangements OK	19
enough information/support	15
employ lots of minority group people	6
company too small	2
employ few minority people	2
can't change things	2
don't know	3
TOTAL	58

Table A13 Firms with equal opportunities policies: provision and need for race relations or equal opportunities training

numbers

Provide RR or EO training	25
No RR or EO training	24
No RR or EO training, but need it	10
No RR or EO training, don't need it	14

Reasons for not needing eo/rr training -
(only those who have no such training in their firm)

not an issue	5
we provide equal opps	3
present arrangements OK	5
enough information/support	5
employ lots of minority group people	1
TOTAL	14

Appendix II: Telephone Interview Schedule

POLICY STUDIES INSTITUTE
RACE RELATIONS TRAINING

Telephone Questionnaire

GENERAL SAMPLE OF EMPLOYERS

Organisation _____

Telephone Number _____

Industry Group (Print-out) _____

Informant's Name _____

Job Title _____

Address _____

_____

_____

Advance information _____

_____

_____

A1.   INTRODUCTION MODULE – SEE CARD A

A2.   QUERIES – SEE QUERY SHEET 1

B.   INDUSTRY

B1.   First, can I ask what your firm makes or does?

_____

_____

C.   TRAINING

C1.   Has any member of staff received any training on procedures for recruitment and selection?

                                        Yes   1
                                        No   2

IF NO, GO TO C3
IF YES –

C2.   Could you give me more details?

   PROMPT: Was it an actual course?

         Did you employ an outside trainer or consultant?

_____

_____

_____

ASK ALL

C3.   Do you arrange for management or administrative staff to have training on any other personnel aspects of their jobs?

                                        Yes   1
                                        No   2

IF NO, GO TO C5
IF YES –

C4.   Could you give me more details?

   PROMPT: Was it an actual course?

         Did you employ an outside trainer or consultant?

_____

_____

_____

ASK ALL

C5.   Have any managers or other employees received any training on employment laws?

                                        Yes   1
                                        No   2

IF NO, GO TO C7
IF YES, CONTINUE WITH C6

C6.   Could you give me more details?

PROMPT: What aspects of the law?

Was it an actual course?

Did you employ an outside trainer or consultant?

_____

_____

_____

ASK ALL

C7.   Have any managers or other employees received any training regarding equal opportunities or race relations?

	Yes	1
	No	2

IF NO, GO TO C9
IF YES –

C8.   Could you give me more details?

PROMPT: Was it an actual course?
Did you employ an outside trainer or consultant?
IF YES – who?
    – were you satisfied or dissatisfied with the training?
    – why? (presentation, style content?)

_____

_____

_____

ASK ALL

C9.   Has your firm ever had any contact with the Department of Employment's Race Relations Advisory Service (RREAS)?

	Yes	1
	No	2

… or with any of the Industrial Language Training Units (ILTs)?

	Yes	1
	No	2

IF NO TO BOTH (RREA AND ILTU), GO TO C11
IF YES TO EITHER, CONTINUE WITH C10

C10. Could you give me more details?

   PROMPT   – what service did they offer?
            – what service did you take up?
            – were you satisfied or dissatisfied with the service?
            – why?

_____

_____

_____

ASK ALL

C11. Do you personally feel that there is any need within your firm for staff
      training in any of the following areas?

	Yes	No
... Selection, recruitment and personnel	1	2
... Employment law	1	2
... Equal opportunities and race relations	1	2

IF YES TO ALL OF THESE, GO TO D1
IF NO TO ANY OF THESE, CONTINUE WITH C12

C12. Could you say why there is no need for staff training in these areas?

      *IF INFORMANT GIVES NO SPECIFIC ANSWER REGARDING EO AND RACE
      RELATIONS, PURSUE ONE*

_____

_____

_____

D.   EQUAL OPPORTUNITIES

D1. Does your firm have a written equal opportunities policy of any sort?

                          Yes   1
                          No   2

IF NO GO TO D6
IF YES CONTINUE WITH D2

D2.　For how long has your firm had the policy?

PROMPT IF NECESSARY: More than a year?

　　　WRITE IN ＿＿＿＿＿＿＿＿＿＿＿＿＿＿＿＿

D3.　How long is the written policy?

PROMPT IF NECESSARY: A paragraph, a page or more?

　　　WRITE IN ＿＿＿＿＿＿＿＿＿＿＿＿＿＿＿＿

D4.　Is any particular employee or manager responsible for overseeing the development and implementation of the policy? Who?

No-one	1
Me	2

Other person
WRITE IN ＿＿＿＿＿＿＿＿＿＿＿＿＿＿＿＿

D5.　Do you know who initiated the original discussions that led to the setting up of the equal opportunities policy?

PROMPT IF NECESSARY: WAs it you, or another manager, or a staff representative, or who?

＿＿＿＿＿＿＿＿＿＿＿＿＿＿＿＿＿＿＿＿＿＿＿＿＿＿＿＿＿＿＿

ASK ALL

D6.　Does your firm keep records of the ethnic origin of employees or job applicants?

Yes	1
No	2

D7.　Has your firm ever had to deal with an industrial tribunal case over race or sex discrimination?

Yes	1
No	2

IF YES – What happened? Was it over race or sex?
RECORD BRIEF DETAILS

＿＿＿＿＿＿＿＿＿＿＿＿＿＿＿＿＿＿＿＿＿＿＿＿＿＿＿＿＿＿＿

＿＿＿＿＿＿＿＿＿＿＿＿＿＿＿＿＿＿＿＿＿＿＿＿＿＿＿＿＿＿＿

D8. Have you heard of the Race Relations Code of Practice produced by the Commission for Racial Equality?

Yes	1
No	2

F NO, GO TO D12
F YES –

D9. To your knowledge, has your firm received a copy of the Code of Practice?

Yes	1
No	2

F NO, GO TO D12
F YES –

D10. Have you looked at it?

Yes	1
No	2

F NO, GO TO D12
F YES –

D11. Have you read through it?

Yes	1
No	2

D12. *CONTINUE WITH D12 AND D13 IF THERE IS NO EQUAL OPPS POLICY*
IF THERE IS A POLICY, SKIP TO SECTION E

Has the issue of equal opportunities, race or sex discrimination ever been brought up for formal discussion by a staff representative, a manager, or anyone else in the firm?

Yes	1
No	2

IF YES –

By whom? _____

What happened? _____

_____

D13. In your view, why is it that the firm has no policy or statement on equal opportunities?

_____

_____

_____

E. CLASSIFICATION SECTION

So that we can compare your answers with those of people in similar situations we would like to ask a few general questions about your firm.

E1. How many establishments are there in your firm in the UK, including your own?

WRITE IN   _____

E2. And how many people are there employed by your firm in the whole of the UK?

WRITE IN   _____

PROMPT WITH RANGES

Under 50	1
50 – 99	2
100 – 199	3
200 – 499	4
500 – 999	5
1000 – 4999	6
5000+	7

E3. How many people are there employed at your establishment?

WRITE IN   _____

PROMPT WITH RANGES

Under 50	1
50 – 99	2
100 – 199	3
200 – 499	4
500 – 999	5
1000 – 4999	6
5000+	7

E4. At your establishment, what proportion of the employees would you say are of minority ethnic origin?

None	1
Under 5 per cent	2
5 – 9 per cent	3
10 – 19 per cent	4
20+ per cent	5

Other answer   _____

E5. Finally , I would like to ask about the methods you use to recruit people for the different types of job in your firm.
How do you usually fill vacancies for ...

... manual jobs?

... counter sales staff?

... office staff?

... management staff?

FILL IN UNPROMPTED ANSWERS THEN PROMPT WITH PRE-CODES 1, 2 and 3
('Do you also ...')

	man ual	cntr sale	off ice	manag ment
No of jobs of this type	0	0	0	0
Adverts in the press	1	1	1	1
Jobcentres or Careers Office	2	2	2	2
Employment agencies	3	3	3	3
Other method(s) *DESCRIBE AND NOTE WHICH JOB TYPE*	4	4	4	4

_____

CODE THESE RESPONSES IF GIVEN BUT DO NOT PROMPT:

Personal recommendation of present staff	5	5	5	5
Unsolicited applications	6	6	6	6
Promotion and internal advertising	7	7	7	7

CLOSE INTERVIEW AND REMIND INFORMANT THAT THEY WILL RECEIVE A LETTER GIVING MORE DETAILS OF THE STUDY. DO NOT FORGET TO THANK INFORMANT FOR HIS OR HER CO-OPERATION

This book is to be returned on
or before the date stamped below

10-6-04

The Policy Studies Institute (PSI) is Britain's leading independent research organisation undertaking studies of economic, industrial and social policy, and the workings of political institutions.

PSI is a registered charity, run on a non-profit basis, and is not associated with any political party, pressure group or commercial interest.

PSI attaches great importance to covering a wide range of subject areas with its multi-disciplinary approach. The Institute's 30+ researchers are organised in teams which currently cover the following programmes:

Family Finances and Social Security
Health Studies and Social Care
Innovation and New Technology
Quality of Life and the Environment
Social Justice and Social Order
Employment Studies
Arts and the Cultural Industries
Information Policy
Education

This publication arises from the Social Justice and Social Order programme and is one of over 30 publications made available by the Institute each year.

Information about the work of PSI, and a catalogue of available books can be obtained from:

Marketing Department, PSI
100 Park Village East, London NW1 3SR